Frozen Grief

A Sister's Story of Grieving Sudden Loss

Frozen Grief

A Sister's Story of Grieving Sudden Loss

Karen Kohler Kaiser

 This book was written by this author to the best of her knowledge regarding truthful events. This is a work of nonfiction. Names, characters, places, brands, media, and incidents are accurate to the best of the author's recollection.

Cover design by Karen Kohler Kaiser

Frozen Grief

A Sister's Story of Grieving Sudden Loss

First edition, Paperback

ISBN No. 978-1484909157

For my sister, Kathy

For my nephew, Kadin

For my mom, Phyllis Kohler

... Save a place for me

Acknowledgments

I would like to thank those closest to me who gave much-needed emotional support during the writing of this book. I cherish you all. My understanding family, Jeff, Erik, Danielle, Zach, and my grandkids that lifted my spirits. Love you!

I would like to thank my dearest friends who never left my side: Tami, Cathie, Lori, and Ed. All my love…

Thank you to my dearest friend and traveling companion, Karen.

Thanks to Wendy whose reading and honest perceptiveness added to the progress of the book. Thanks to Proof Positive Papers and my editor, Cindy.

To all my family, cousins, friends, and church
who prayed… unceasingly.

Contents

Foreword

Tyler Sparks, licensed counselor

Grieving is a lot like storytelling. It has a beginning that can sometimes be shocking and daunting; a middle, that can sometimes get muddled, confusing, and detailed; and an end that may have closure but can stick with the reader long after the final page has been turned.

Storytelling is an important aspect of grief work and parallels the horrible, yet healing, process of embracing the loss of loved ones, the finality of this life, and our own limitedness.

Karen Kaiser, in her work, *Frozen Grief,* has captured the shock and horror that unfolds when receiving the devastating news that someone has died and the long, slow journey to finding peace in the midst of pain. She comes at this subject from an experiential perspective that leads the reader to be consoled by her story. Readers will not find in this book trite responses or overused phrases that bring false comfort. Instead, they will be offered a window into the harsh reality of a life that has been stained by traumatic deaths but has not suffered defeat.

Through her eyes, readers get a bird's eye view of someone who is sometimes at peace, sometimes in tears, sometimes angry, sometimes "crazy," and sometimes fighting against suppressing emotions.

Be reassured by these words from Lamentations—a book in the Bible dedicated to mourning and grief:

> For the Lord will not
> cast off forever,
> but, though he cause grief, he will have
> compassion
> according to the abundance of
> steadfast love;
> for he does not afflict from his heart
> or grieve the children of men.
> Lamentations 3:31-33

My prayer for you, reader, is that you are comforted by Karen's story and are able to make sense of your experiences as you embrace the pain of losing someone.

Tyler Sparks is a licensed counselor and co-owner of CarePoint Christian Counseling in Kirkwood, Missouri. He considers it part of his calling and privilege as a counselor to walk alongside those who are grieving and make sense of the overwhelming emotions after someone has experienced loss. To find out more about CarePoint Christian Counseling please visit www.CarePointCounseling.com.

Introduction

"My grief lies all within, and these external manners of lament are merely shadows to the unseen grief that swells with silence in the tortured soul." ~ William Shakespeare

I chose to remain frozen in my grief…

What's more, I refused to thaw my feelings and go through further emotional pain until I was ready!

No, staying frozen with my feelings, in an indeterminate state, gave my mind a chance to settle. I was not ready for my loved ones to depart suddenly from this life, and I surely had not been forewarned that they would be leaving forever. It was not as if they had experienced a long, painful illness, giving me time to mentally brace myself for their death-if that's even possible. I was not given opportunity to prepare, not even for a second, for anyone's passing. Nope, my implausible tragedy was dreadfully abrupt. I was mentally powerless, my mind was blown, and I had accepted that as fact.

But, if I were going to go through agonizing and resurrecting intense pain during my grieving process, grief journey, or grief stages, as it has been described to me, then it would be a full grief response …this time.

I did not want to be pressured or feel the anxiety to be rushed along or forced into grieving on a distinct timeline. Given our fast paced society, you may find as I did, grieving isn't given sufficient magnitude. Speeding through is almost expected or else you may find yourself yoked with a professionally diagnosis. I wanted, at the very least, to have control of when I would give myself the permission to feel wretched and grieve. Furthermore, perhaps selfishly, I wanted to take as much time as I needed to heal the gaping gash in my heart from this deep pain.

When you experience the tragic death of someone close, your initial thoughts focus on recollecting the last time you saw the dearly departed alive. Was the last time you heard their voice in a phone conversation? Did you see them in person just a few days earlier or maybe weeks ago? How about seeing them in the flesh just a few short hours or minutes prior to their death, when everything was very much OK.

You'll find your thoughts rapidly review past events in an attempt to process the final moments, both good and possibly not so good, with your loved one. Your brain instantly pulls those precious last images together as you hopelessly try to make sense of the untimely death.

Even extreme thoughts, perhaps of the agony they may have experienced in their last moments, bash painfully about in your psyche as your mind tries unsuccessfully to slow down the bombardment of unpleasant images. Perhaps as a protective measure, the brain attempts to focus and slow those images in an effort to lessen the emotional trauma.

In the aftermath of one's own life, now very much altered by sudden death of loved ones, kind-hearted souls express to you that "time heals all wounds." I'm not sure time heals ALL wounds, all the pain of loss, but it does lessen in intensity throughout the years. The loss remains, and few words bring immediate thaw to the pain.

Someone who has tragically stomached loss would be more appreciative to hear "I've maybe not been where you are, but I'm here if you need to talk, or cry."

Even when others offered comfort to me, I was callous that I had experienced such a personally deep, distressing loss and unwisely discounted that comfort they freely gave. If grief's wretchedness was a trial that would eventually make me stronger then I would be guilty of being a horrible griever. Convict me; go ahead and sentence me to limitless days of aloneness, sorrow, and sadness because I felt absolutely frozen in spirit.

What I have heard from others who have lost someone suddenly is that they justly grieve not having the opportunity to say goodbye face to face before their loved ones died. Strategies for coping are debilitated as you may be inconsolable.

* * *

When my 72-year-old grandmother had a stroke, she was in the hospital for several weeks before her body failed her and she passed away. During that month, I was able to rationalize and start accepting that my grandmother may not make it through this stroke - she might die. My grandmother was somewhat responsive after her stroke. Speech was arduous, but she could squeeze my hand and acknowledged my presence. As her condition deteriorated, I believe in my heart she heard me say goodbye and that she knew I loved her as I stayed by her bedside as she lay dying. I grieved the loss of my grandmother in a very different way than those I lost without warning.

People who have experienced sudden loss and have had guilt involving the deceased may have more difficult time mourning. Enter self-reproach because of words or events not adequately resolved when they were alive. I sincerely did not have any guilty regrets. I just was not ready to make the intense effort required to start to heal-it would take work yielding to grieve.

I did, however, put effort into letting my still-living loved ones know how much they meant to me and that I hoped they always would see I truly loved them with all my heart.

Still, even with the confidence of knowing my living family realized how much they meant to me, losing someone close from a sudden death was a deeply intense shock to my physical and mental health, as it is for most people. Unattended death may bring with it unanswered questions that leaves the griever yearning for the answers.

Questions such as:

"Why did they die?" or

"When or how exactly did they die?" or

"Did they suffer?"

Irrational thinking and the "what ifs" can also enter into play and take a place in front of the line with all the processing going on during this overwhelming, sudden, mind-blow, overload-post-death.

Ultimately, having the faith that our loved ones are at peace in paradise, in the presence of our Lord, understandably gives us strength and weakens grief's grip. Still, we may never completely get over the tragic loss of a loved one. We just accept.

Good-hearted people around constantly asked how I was "doing," and the question was distressing to me. I knew how I *really* was doing, but I tried to be polite and said I was "fine," even though I was smothering inside and miserable. I was lying when I said I was fine, and that caused me even more inner turmoil.

I have seen a number of counselors and psychiatrists in an effort to get a grasp on grief, and, from my experience, the professionals' grief philosophies vary greatly. Shortly after my sudden loss, I asked my then psychiatrist what response would be appropriate to people who asked how I was doing, since I wasn't really "fine." Saying I was "fine" seemed to be the desirable answer. However, I was indeed struggling with answering I was fine. The psychiatrist suggested I tell anyone who asked me how I was doing to respond,

"Aw, that's in my past, I've gotten over that and have moved on."

Since my loss was very fresh, his words were jaw- dropping, so bitter and cold. Even now, I can say I've never fully gotten over his response. I vowed never to return to a psychiatrist again because they didn't understand. However, I would eventually find that my vow to not seek another psychiatrist would be broken. But I never used my first psychiatrist's hard comeback.

I have learned how to travel on the uncomfortable road toward healing. You may also be struggling with intense grief and uneasy about discovering how to adjust and begin healing. But with others help, prayer, and the passing of time, you will begin to acknowledge and accept a post trauma-changed you.

Frozen Grief was written to give courage to grievers who go through a more convoluted grief, a grief that makes no sense and leaves one with unanswered questions that may never be adequately answered.

I truly felt very alone as a sibling survivor frozen in my sudden grief. This is my story.

Portent of a Tragedy

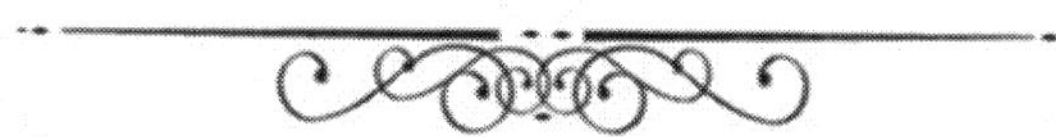

"You gain strength, courage and confidence by every experience in which you really stop to look fear in the face. You are able to say to yourself, 'I have lived through this horror. I can take the next thing that comes along.' You must do the thing you think you cannot do."
~ Eleanor Roosevelt / first lady

When I turned 40 years old in December, two friends and I decided to celebrate our 40th year of life by jumping off a boat dock into freezing - cold river water on New Year's Day. Once we bravely took the plunge, we would become part of a very distinctive group –The Polar Bear Club.

To explain just how cold the water was, especially when one is wearing only a swimsuit in the middle of winter is arduous. There is really no way to prepare for the unexpected shock of the intense cold water on your skin. When your body first hits freezing water, your body experiences what is called a cold-water response. What happens is you take a big gasp because of the unanticipated shocking cold water. Knowing that this response is to be expected can begin to prepare you to not take a mouthful of icy water down to your lungs. I would try to remember that important tip as I jumped and then went under the water as I most surely did not want to drown.

We went to the frozen river and learned the yearly ritual was to jump right off the boat dock into the frigid water, taking the Polar Bear Plunge. Sure sounded simple enough.

This frankly, was a ceremony of sorts, as a line formed on the dock of people of all ages deciding to take the cold-water plunge. Participants exposed their individuality through showy body paintings, wearing frilly tutus, or choosing to jump fully clothed. We anxiously awaited our turn as a man with a microphone asked each person who approached the river why he or she wanted to jump into freezing-cold water.

"We turned 40," my friends and I said in unison, this was reason enough for us to jump.

After the gathered crowd counted aloud 1-2-3…we three leaped off the dock…SPLASH!

I recollect the sound of my body's weighty thud and the audible icy splashes as we went in. Waters cold shards pricked at my unprotected skin. Down I descended from my plunge into the murky water and I waited to float to the top, and it seemed quite a long time. I opened my eyes and saw little through the water's cloudy green color. When you see blackness overhead from under the water, this is the exit opening through the bitter water when there is an ice layer. A visible white color is actually a solid ice sheet.

I had jumped far off the dock. At the time, I didn't think at all about the swim back to the dock. Jumping far meant I would need to swim more to get back to the pier and out of the iced water. My two smart friends were closer.

Once my head bobbed up, I instantly acknowledged how cold the water was. It was hard to catch a breath and my breathing was labored, shallow, and rapid. I was almost gasping. My extremities didn't want to move but I kept thinking, "Let's get to the dock! MOVE legs and arms." My heart was racing. I could feel its rhythmic beat inside me. My swim to the side was more of a dog paddle trying to keep my arms and legs close to my center, where my body knew instinctively they needed to be for me to stay warm.

Escaping the water was difficult because every part of me struggled. Once I exited and was on the dock. I realized my body was oddly almost dry. My skin felt warmer than the cold air. The wintry water repelled off my body much like a duck, I suppose, exiting a pond.

I often think of that crazy frigid jump that I *chose* to take. I can say it haunts me now. I can only begin to conceive how drowning in cold water must feel like as your body fights to survive.

PART

I

The Heartbreak

CHAPTER 1

In the Still of the Night

Ever has it been that love knows not its own depth until the hour of separation.

- Khalil Gibran poet/artist

My cell phone, which was charging bedside, jived loudly, my music ring tone awakening me. "Really, my alarm was not set" was my first thought as I quickly opened my eyes. The familiar '70s disco tune *Ring my Bell* shrilled the alert of an incoming phone call as the song's chorus played on. The bedroom was dark, and the only illumination came from the tiny phone's dim digits and the nearby alarm clock's red numbers glowing the time. I could not help but notice it was showing just before 12.00 a.m.

Through the darkness, I unhurriedly rolled over to my left side in bed and decided to take a quick glance at the phone number that had disturbed my restful sleep. Jostling items on the nightstand, I eventually found the phone resting upon my Bible.

I had been painting on canvas before retiring to bed so my fatigued fingers fumbled to retrieve the cell phone. The unlock button at the top of the device became fully lit as I continued to half grasp the phone's rubbery casing. The bright screen made me squint to focus on the number left unanswered. Still holding the cell phone, my eyes slowly blinked at the unknown number on the display once more as the cell phone's lit screen went dark.

Not falling back asleep just yet, I mused, "Who would be calling in the middle of the night anyway?" I contemplated further as I turned back in the bed. Tucking the downy comforter once again around my body, I anticipated drifting back to a cozy winter slumber. "But, I don't recognize this long string of numbers at all." I was coming to realize, in my sleepy stupor, that the numerals were definitely not a known contact of mine.

"Hum," and with a bit of antipathy, I chalked the call up to nothing more than a misdialed number. The phone returned to the night table to continue charging with the still-unfamiliar number on its face.

With my head on my pillow, I rhythmically counted the seconds in my head until I was sweetly dreaming once more. Dreaming, though, would once again be put on hold, as the cheery chime from the cell phone broke the room's silence and alerted me there was a voicemail.

Annoyed, I took in a deep breath and gave a long, slow sigh as I reached once again for the phone re-concealed in the darkness. The more I thought about the ill-timed disturbance, the more aggravated I was. This time I grabbed the phone and decided to at least half-listen to the new message. I allowed the phone to barely make contact with my ear so the incomplete sentences I was half hearing made little logic to my weary mind.

An instructive message from the St. Clair County Sheriff's Department quickly mustered my dozy mind to a red alert state as I caught the words - Sister…boys… missing…

Missing? What does missing mean? I listened again to the message left on the voicemail much more attentively than the first time and quickly returned the call to the sheriff's department at the number provided. The police officer, in his monotone voice, told me that my sister and the boys' whereabouts were unknown.

The police wanted to know if I had heard from them or if they were by chance with me. "No," I answered, "they are not with me," I knew my sister, Kathy, nephew Kadin and his good friend Austin were to see a movie last night in celebration of Kadin's 7th birthday. The officer told me they were making phone calls and paging their names at area movie theaters to no avail.

I ended the call and was ready to act because something felt wrong, very wrong. I jumped out from beneath the covers and grabbed the new jogging suit my sister had just given me for my birthday. I got dressed hurriedly and put on a pair of running shoes I found by my bed. Simultaneously, I began in haste, telling my now-awake husband what was going on. I told him I had to get to my sister's, now! In record time, we were fully alert, dressed, and driving.

My sister's country home was less than 15 minutes away from mine, which was fortunate as I wanted to be at her home as quickly as possible. I was extremely troubled and confused by how my sister and the boys had gone missing, especially at this time of night. I was trying to ruminate just what the statement "gone missing" meant.

But far worse than the utter confusion, was an intense and unrelenting feeling of dread that was all consuming inside me. "Jeff, you have to drive faster!" I frantically screamed and urged my husband to push the gas pedal to get us to their home in record time. While he focused on safely speeding, I had all the car windows down, letting in the frigid night air, while I shouted their names into the darkness as loud as I could.

"Where are you?"

..."K A T H Y"... "K A D I N"

I screamed at a panicked pitch. My voice traveled through the static air over the open fields. We swiftly drove on the curvy country roads with my head popping in and out of the car's open window. I could hear the thin layer of road chat crackle and crunch as the tires rapidly turned over them. All I could indistinctly recognize in the darkness was harvested farmland that lined the road with dots of lights from farmhouses faintly visible in the distance.

As our car approached her home, we could see brighter lights flashing in the distance. Fire trucks were arriving at the scene and proceeding up the rock drive leaving a dusty trail in the dark. "Why were fire trucks here?" "Was her house on fire?" was my alarmed assessment.

We brought the car to an abrupt halt and left it on the side of the main road. Other cars, none recognizable to me, were arriving. Exiting the car quickly, we raced toward the driveway's chaos. A police officer had his car angled in the grass at the road's entry. I ran to him first, bombarding him with frantic questions but was given few answers. My husband walked directly toward the lights afar to find out what was happening.

My body reacted instinctively, allowing me to sprint. Panicked, I wasted no time and darted around the property's periphery and up the mile-long driveway. Tall leafless trees, with their thorny underbrush, lined the right side of the gravel driveway making a tunnel of arching trees straining to bend to the left side of the rocky road. There was only a sliver of moonlight overhead for a source of illumination, but my eyes night vision quickened and soon fully adjusted to the darkness. I watched for any stirring shadows in the dimness and listened for sounds of movement with heightened senses.

I went off-road from the driveway and could hear the brittle crunch of earth and smell dirt from the farm fields as I hurriedly scuttled over the top soil, disturbing its winter rest.

The house sat on 33 acres of land so there was much ground to cover to find the missing three. Outbuildings and sheds on-site needed exploring. The landscape consisted of a larger lake and a pond, but smaller streams ran about the property restricting access by wild thickets of undergrowth. Surrounding Kathy's home were gates and fences that lined the grassy horse pastures. A large stable and outdoor arena was down a steeper incline from the home, which sat above overlooking the horses, pastures, and water bodies. Kathy's home, a cute white-cottage ranch, has a covered walkway separating the home from a large detached garage. Wrap around porches are on the front and the rear of the home which offer unobstructed views over the pastures and the stable.

But then the rest of the acreage is mostly large dense trees. I considered they may all have gone looking for one of the dogs, which ran into the woods or maybe one of the stabled horses was on the loose. I assuredly told myself I knew the terrain better than the rescuers and would find them. I **had** to find them.

I frantically screamed into the heavy night air,

"Kathy!

"Kadin!"

"Boys!"

"Where are you? "

" Answer!"

"It's me, Karen!"

"God, where are they?!"

No reply.

While running aimlessly, I continued my pleading shouting frenzy - darting through the winter woodland of thick leaves underfoot and naturally fallen trees. I was slowed only by catching my clothes on prickly sticks that were invisible in the darkness. Surely if my sister was trapped, fell, or twisted her ankle she would hear me in panic and respond. But she didn't.

Even with no audible response, I kept running in search of them. All the while I was formulating what rescue scenarios may be soon needed.

I moved my frantic hunt to another hardened field, then to a curvilinear stream bed hidden in the wood. I spotted a beam of light in the distance swinging back and forth through the night like a pendulum on an antique grandfather clock. The light quickly turned to focus on me and I could hear the men's outcry "Kathy, Kathy." I could make out moving silhouettes and determined it must be firefighters walking the fields, as I was, looking for them. In the distance they began shouting at me "Kathy" as if I were she. I shouted back.

"No, "

"I'm Karen, Kathy's sister."

The rescuers had detected me with a device that gave thermal readings. My body was now sweat drenched in an energy-burning pursuit to find my family, so I imagined the thermal reading was a red fireball ablaze on the machines screen.

It seemed I was interfering with their methodical search efforts by taking on my own pursuit. I instinctively changed course, because the searchers obviously had this area of her property covered and headed toward the house. I did not pause, however, from my own search mission.

Turning, I could see more clearly the flashing, twirling lights filtering through woody trees and branches. Deeply indented gravel, pressed by the tires of the heavy rescue trucks, made a trough for me to run up an incline and around the corner to the house. I ran closer to the lights and passed first by the small pond, which was in the front of the house.

Gasping, I was immediately caught off guard as I caught sight of more rescue vehicles, from several nearby towns, lining the levee driveway. The trucks had parked bumper-to-bumper all with their red lights steadily beaming into the dark countryside.

Unrestricted, I found my way around the flurry of lights and activity and headed straight toward the house. I felt warmed heat penetrate my clothes from the running engines and smelled fuel exhaust heavy in the air as I passed by the assembly. Men in full protective gear moved about. When I saw the mighty cavalry assembled, I was sure with all the available work force we could comb the entire vicinity and quickly locate them.

CHAPTER 2

All God's Creatures

The reason it hurts so much to separate is because our souls are connected.

-Nicholas Sparks, author

On the way up to the house, I met my dad, Richard, and stepmom, Dorothy. They had received a similar unsettling wake-up call about the same time as Jeff and I. At the top of the small hill, close by the house, the family thronged together. I had paused from my personal search now because I desperately wanted to speak directly with my brother-in-law.

Finding him in the huddle, I hugged him tightly and saw his obvious state of total shock. "Please, tell me everything up till now," I begged. Slowly, and in a low voice he fed me bits of information. The details he gave were in the form of a timeline leading up to when they were considered to be missing.

He said it was already dark when he arrived home. As he was driving his work truck up the driveway to the house, he said he noticed my sister's short lace-up boots, a glove, and her coat lying along the levee of the pond in front of the house. I immediately thought it appeared as though my sister was trying to leave a trail to follow. I interrupted my brother-in-law. "Do they think they were abducted?" He did not respond. He continued with his narrative of events, his eyes glazed and fixed.

He went on to say sadly that he did not think anything was out of sorts when he noticed my sister's items lying about as their pet dogs sometimes drag around items while playing. He moved the coat, glove, and boots to the porch. After working a long day, my brother- in- law went into the house and went to sleep for the night without any concerns as he rises for work early in the mornings. He set the ringer on his phone to "off" before he lay down to go to sleep. He knew they were seeing a movie at the theater for my nephew's birthday, and would be returning home afterward because Kathy had called him earlier and told him he would be home before they would.

Kadin's older brother, Keegan, remained at home and was unaware of any mishap with their leaving for the movie. He had already settled into his room for the night knowing his dad was arriving shortly.

Kadin's friend, Austin, was to be picked up by his mother, at the theater, after the movie was over. My sister texted frequently on her phone, so for Kathy not to contact his mom and update was peculiar. Once Kathy and the boys failed to meet up with Austin's parents after the movie, his mom tried to call Kathy at their home phone number and cell phones. No answer.

"So where are they?" "Where could they be?" I anxiously pleaded with my brother-in- law.

My sister drives a luxury extended truck that is equipped with a satellite OnStar package. The police found out more information about the vehicle's whereabouts that evening by checking with the service. "Great," I thought to myself. "If they had car trouble, or an accident, or ran off the road somewhere then they can locate exactly where they are."

To my surprise, I learned the investigators had already discovered her vehicle and thankfully had been no car accident. The truck had not moved from home. It was still in the detached garage with Kathy's purse inside and the keys in the ignition. Kathy's cell phone was inside the house on the kitchen counter.

I offered up some possibilities. "Maybe Kathy forgot her phone and used another purse?" Or, possibly, "Her mother-in-law, Carol, had decided to go along and drive. They might have stopped for a bite to eat, or changed plans at the last minute," I suggested as I stood there. "Then where ARE they? It is late in the evening, and surely they would be home for cake and ice cream by now." I continued on. My brother-in-law was in such shock he could not go on further with our conversation. He puckered his lips tight together as if holding back tears. His eyes were wide and full of fear.

Jeff approached me while I mentally sifted through the information. He said he had called and talked with our pastor and asked him for prayer. Our pastor was on his way to my sister's house.

My husband said he had talked with the investigators on the scene. It became instantly quiet.

I could tell he had something pressing he wanted to tell me. "What does he need to say to me?" I looked at him worriedly. With a horror-struck look, he held my shoulders as if trying to steady himself. "Tell me." I recoiled, not sure, if I was ready to know more. Choking out a few comprehensible syllables, I couldn't catch what he was trying to say, but grasped a few words as they broke apart by the now-rasping tone of his voice.

My husband was trying to explain why the trucks and extra-large spot lights were lining the driveway and why two ambulances were also stationed there.

Actually, all the equipment on the levee was no longer intended for a searching and rescue anymore, but horribly worse – they were bracing for a recovery.

"They think Kathy and the boys are in the lake," my husband choked out.

I bellowed "No, No, No, No….NO!" at the top of my lungs. "God, please NO." I pleaded that what my husband was telling me just couldn't be true!

The first responders on the scene must have been waiting for me to receive the horrifying news. The hectic movement of men over the area, had somewhat slowed and groups of rescuers formed huddled groups in between warm, still-running trucks. My search efforts were all in vain from the start.

The true reality of the situation was that the authorities were trying to find and recover my only sister, Kathy, my nephew Kadin and his close friend Austin's bodies from the icy pond water.

My body froze with fear - the world stopped. Countless things ran through my mind, but the love I held inside my heart for them was pounding in panic. My first reaction was "I'm going in." I will save them. They must be saved!" My family understood the pain but held me back trying to talk a moment of sense into me. There was no sense in this situation. I surged toward the pond, attempting to get near the water, only to be restrained by the rescuers on the scene.

"They don't understand!" I repeated several times over. "They can't understand?" I thought. I stood powerless.

The magnitude of the horrible tragedy completely overwhelmed me. Somehow my mind exchanged this terrifying scene to beget a happier thought of how life was just earlier this week…

The doorbell rang at my home, and it was my sister Kathy visiting. She had stopped by on a gloomy winter day to help me acclimate to my new puppy. I had wanted a basset hound pup since high school. However, the timing never seemed right. Finally, after many years I finally had my own puppy.

Kathy had been an animal lover since she was a little girl. Our childhood home was located just at the city limits of our small town and we would find stray animals wandering our way. Kindhearted Kathy would befriend homeless dogs, rabbits, and reptiles, if they managed to make their way to our house without an identity collar. She would give the new pet a name as if they were her very own to keep. A couple of the stray dogs I recall by name - Jumper, a German shepherd, and Dottie (aptly named) was a colorful beagle mix, while others fade from memory. We already had two live-in pet dogs - Angel, a white poodle, and our fierce watchdog Chihuahua, Cuddles.

For the befriended animals, sleeping arrangements were usually in the garage, unless Kathy could sneak them into the house. Otherwise, the dogs had a comfortable bed made of folded towels in a makeshift doghouse, constructed of cardboard, hand decorated with crayons and markers by my sister. Kathy also designed turtle shoeboxes or resurrected sturdier metal cages vacated by the former inhabitants. Thankfully, the latest edition of *The World Book Encyclopedia* provided helpful information on the care and food for her zoo. Mealtime for her company consisted of meaty or leafy leftovers slipped straight from the dinner table.

I cringed when my sister, as an adult, had Leo, a gecko. Leo the lizard had a warming lamp and ate crickets-the live black kind, while resting atop a rock. She would go to the local bait shop and pick up the gecko gourmet treats. One thing I knew for sure, my sister loved caring for all God's creatures. Kathy even managed to get herself a job at a local animal hospital when she was older - feeding her needs to nurture.

"Oh, she is so cute," my sister had said about my new pup. Kathy couldn't wait to see my puppy, Dalilah. She wanted my pup to come over to her house to play with her new fox terrier puppy, Pasha, her newest addition. Pasha would need to make friends with Zena, her Welsh corgi, and a female cat-Thomas. Kadin named the cat Thomas. It stayed named Thomas.

While I had dreams of a little hound puppy as a child, my sister was dreaming of her much bigger animal dream - galloping on horseback. Kathy's love made absolutely no sense since we lived in town, not in the country, and were seldom even around any horses.

Nevertheless, my sister made her dream into a reality when she was an adult. She sought to find other horse lovers, learned the ropes so to speak, and then successfully boarded horses for a living at her own barn, Saddle Creek Stables. Kathy told me, "When you find something you love, don't give up on it, even if you haven't the faintest idea how to do it." That was the case with Kathy. She never gave up on her dreams. But now my sister and her son and his friend would have no more dreams to fulfill.

CHAPTER 3

Taking Control of Tragedy

God's promises are like the stars; the darker the night the brighter they shine–

David Nicholas author

Since no bodies were yet recovered from the water, there was still a glimmer of hope that perhaps not all three perished. I held out for that hope. Maybe Kathy or the boys or even just one of the boys were so terrified they were hiding somewhere to be still found alive.

Emotionally fraught, I needed to flee, escape the recovery turmoil, even for a short time, so I could do some thinking alone. The woods around the pond provided a vantage point for me to somewhat hide from view and watch the ongoing efforts to find them. Now, distanced far enough away from the scene, I managed to focus and shut everything out to come to the realization that I was gazing upon my hell on earth.

Soon though, by myself, I returned to a full state of panic, and I couldn't process what was real or imagined. I was on complete overload, and my body instinctively shut out what was not essential, perhaps some divine protective measure of the human body in crisis. It was as if I could no longer perform two motor functions at once. As I was listening to the commotion from my woodsy vantage point, I had to have my eyes closed to focus on hearing what was said. With my eyes open seeing the shocking scene -it was as if my ears would not function to hear at the same time and I had become deaf.

Seizing my cell phone, I started to call friends to share in my tragedy. Oddly, one of my friends said she had her phone next to her on her nightstand before she went to sleep because she for some reason felt I would be calling. With rushed words, bordering on incoherence, I gasped to get air in my lungs fast enough to get the words out. "Kathy… Kadin and his friend… drowned." "How can I live without them, HOW?" I called others friends, who should have been asleep, and they listened on the line to my horrendous account.

I must have been screaming loudly because the concerned investigators met me in the thick of the woods and wanted to usher me into the house so I did not experience what most people could not even begin to bear. They also requested that the rest of the family wait inside the house, out of direct view, and stay where it was warm. The police promised they would come in the house and give immediate updates to the family.

I knew for any peace of mind I had left I needed to be watching the events unfold no matter the temperature. Oddly, the freezing February temperatures did not seem to affect my body. I was actually hot and perspiring as I camped out in those woods. The detectives told me again it was not something I needed to see. I held my ground and did not move from the woods. "I just can't leave," I held.

I returned to the earlier notion of how I wanted so badly to just jump in and try to find them, save them, recover them if they indeed were underwater. Heightened emotions mixed with coursing adrenalin are a combination that caused me to have grandiose ideas as the immensity of the horrific situation overtook me.

The entire scene was like watching a scripted television drama, only this was real-life tragedy happening to our family. I couldn't even think to leave them, wherever they were, and I wasn't going to leave willingly no matter how many people tried to convince me otherwise.

In my heart, until a body was recovered, I still had hope.

With dark tree branches, fallen logs and underbrush the only visible obstructers for my full on horrific view, I saw the bright searchlights focusing to illuminate an entry point of blackness through the ice on the pond. Broken ice pieces floated over the dark water. A rope was strung from the pond bank to a tree across to the other side of the water creating a straight line above. The overhead rope guided a yellow inflated raft, which held a few men and assisted divers in the frigid water, who floated ready to continue the submerged search. I could see everyone's breath in the cold night air rise like puffs of smoke from a cozy chimney.

Men plunged long metal poles into the water and maneuvered the raft. These poles churned floating ice and swirled the water beneath all in hopes of hooking the bodies below. Oddly, the ominous scene was rather quiet. I could hear the water stir underneath the raft as they meticulously inched over the icy pond. Other than the agitating of frozen water, I did not notice any verbal responses or instructions from the rescuers. Very little was said.

By the frozen waters bank along the driveway and up to the icy entry point further out on the little lake, footsteps showed the pounding prints of frantic running. These footsteps beat a straight path upon the thin ice as it gave way underfoot reaching the ice opening,

"Were these my sister's last steps taken on earth?" Horror filled me as I imagined the heart-wrenching last moments my sister and the boys endured.

I felt like the rescue was going so slow. I wanted to assist in the efforts to urgently find them. What felt like hours of passing time were in reality just seconds on the clock. Restless, I returned to the somber hill by the house and embraced close friends who had made their way to the unfolding scene. These friends shouldered my unbearable pain.

I felt helpless… absolutely helpless, and desperate. I understood that the investigators had a job to do, and I hadn't intended to become a problem for them. But because I was so close to my sister and nephew, I couldn't imagine not being a part of their last moments.

"I'll jump in and help find them. I'm not afraid," I told my friends, family, and the rescuers yet again. "I know what cold water is like!" But not being granted permission to be nearer the water and the recovery mission made me increasingly and uncontrollably irate, despite my pleading from friends and family. To get closer to the water, to the ice, I tried to break through a barricade of men positioned to keep me out of the way. I hysterically darted back and forth as if running a football play to get closer. I knew my goal, and I just had to break through the line of men. When my efforts failed, I was sacked and stopped. I looked one of the investigators in the eyes and said,

"This is **my** tragedy. If I'm not there as soon as she's recovered or if I don't get to see my sister when you find her, you'll have to live with denying me that request to see her for the rest of your life!"

He looked at me with concerned sympathy and promised if they recovered her, I could see her. I believed him. They reassured me and stopped me from becoming a possible casualty.

Relaxing my posture a bit, I looked skyward and noticed small twinkles of stars far removed from what was happening on earth. With watered eyes closed, I shut out all that was going on around me now to spend time pleading with God.

"Why take them now ...WHY?"

After all, Kadin and his friend were just little boys, and Kathy was all that remained of my mother here on earth. God knew all of this and he knew all my past scars from profound hurts. While I was deep in thought with frantic prayers, I was taken back to a time when I had desperately prayed and pleaded for our mom to live - more than 20 years earlier.

* * *

CHAPTER 4

Mom Remembered

I remember my mother's prayers and they have always followed me. They have clung to me all my life. - *Abraham Lincoln*

It was a summer day in the Midwest and a great day for my little sister and me to play on our swing set in the backyard. While we played carefree, my mother spent time sitting in the sun, watching over us. I remember how my mom's skin would suntan easily into a beautiful dark tone when she spent time outside. Likewise, my sister Kathy and her two boys were blessed with bronze complexions.

Mom also had the deepest of brown (near-black) hair color that Kathy and her boys also boasted. Mom used to tell us the dark skin and dark hair was from Native American blood somewhere in our ancestry.

On the other hand, as a fair-skinned child myself, with skin more like my father's, I would turn a bright red, blister, and peel when I spent time in the sun.

On this particular sunny day, while Kathy and I played outside, mom experienced something she believed was supernatural.

Mom waited to tell us her "secret experience" from that sunny day until we were in our teens. She told Kathy and me, "Don't tell anyone what I tell you because they will think you are both crazy." What my mother told us then which she thought others would not believe, has given me great comfort and a different outlook on death and dying now as I treasure her encounter.

Here follows what my mother believed best I should keep to myself.

While Kathy and I played in our sandbox, she was lying relaxed on a beach towel on the back porch .Mom felt a calm breeze peacefully blow over her. She recollected looking up at the line of pine trees behind our house only to notice the air she felt on her skin was more- deliberate. The wind was tranquil, and the trees did not move in any way from the airstream. She told us how odd and unexplainable it was to feel such a current of air with nothing else at all moving. Untroubled, she lay down once again to soak up the warmth of the sun.

She told us shortly after she experienced the calm breeze she heard a very clear voice out of nowhere…speak. This concealed voice came, she believed, from the wind.

She was not frightened of the breeze or the voice, which she recalled as having a gentle, deeper male tone. The voice said to her, "You will be very sick. Do not do what the doctors want you to do." Then the soothing voice and the tranquil breeze left her. She felt that voice she heard was a messenger as she looked back at that moment some time later.

Six months passed and she did indeed become sick as the voice foretold- sick with cancer.

Mom told us the specialists wanted her to have all her lymph nodes surgically removed to rid her body of the cancer. Mom, after recalling the insightful voice in the wind, told the doctors… no, she would not let them remove all her lymph nodes. The stunned doctors were very displeased with Mom's decision to ignore their recommended treatment. They wanted her to seriously think about the dire consequences of not doing the surgery and leaving a husband and two small girls without a mother. She still said… no.

The faith my mother must have had in the power behind the voice, to hear it and obey, even if it meant death, to go against the doctors' requests is remarkable testimony. Her conviction to fully trust in something bigger gives personal strength to me in my Christian walk, as she is an ongoing exemplar to me.

Realizing my mother would not move from her decision against surgery, the cancer doctors approached her with another option. This alternative course of therapy was somewhat new on the cancer frontier, so mom would be taking an enormous chance with its effectiveness to cure her cancer. Mom said she prayed and then agreed to become a research subject for experimental treatments for her type of cancer, Hodgkin's disease. By choosing the non- traditional treatment, her therapy did not require that her lymph nodes be removed. The treatment she received was high doses of Cobalt 60 radiation and chemotherapy.

There were side effects from her treatment, bad side effects. I recall during much of my childhood my mom was generally fatigued and napped often. She had a long scar on the top of her feet, which remained raised, from where they administered the Cobalt treatments. As a child I remembered seeing the mark and thinking of Jesus. He on the cross during crucifixion, in agony, with a spike in his feet - that is what I thought my mom was feeling. I would sit in church and stare at the cross with Jesus and see his suffering and think of my mommy's suffering.

Her immune system was forever compromised from all the treatments so she became ill easily when exposed to someone ailing. I remember her losing her beautiful hair rather quickly, so she wore wigs. Kathy and I had lots of playtime and pageantry as we modeled her assortments of up-do and frosted wigs that sat atop a white Styrofoam shaped head so they could be easily styled.

Mom's natural teeth weakened and were removed as a result of her treatments so she wore first an upper and later a lower set of full dentures to replace her lost smile. She was so self-conscious of those false teeth. We rarely saw her without them. She had a difficult time speaking because her saliva glands were so damaged by the radiation treatments that she was afflicted with little saliva flow, which produced severe dry mouth.

Even with the lack of moisture in Mom's mouth and her chronic fatigue, she always managed to smile at Kathy and me and all the quirky kid things we would do to amuse her.

Perhaps seeing my mom and her deteriorated teeth at her young age inspired me to help save teeth and give comfort to those going through mouth pain. I entered the dental field in 1986 and am currently a registered dental hygienist.

Mom also told of apparitions. These angel beings visited her several times when she was in the hospital with her cancer. She described them as misty lighted forms, which visited her during her sickest and toughest times. They said to her, "It's time to go. You can come now." Mom said she had several visits with them, and they told her it was her time. Each time she heard them she replied,

"No, please let me stay long enough to raise my little girls." Mom repeated her plea.

"Please let me raise my girls!" The voices left her.

My mom's cancer went into remission and she lived to raise her girls.

Mom had a diverse religious background. She was born Lutheran, confirmed into faith as a Protestant, and married and converted to Roman Catholicism. We were raised Catholic.

Sunday mornings would arrive at our house, and she made sure her girls were well-presented for church. Mom seldom made it to mass with us. It was hard on her body's lowered immune system to be around a group of people and when she would get ill, she'd stay sick for days.

The night before church, mom would hand roll and bobby pin (hard rollers were much too agonizing for sleeping) our hair so our long banana curls would be ready for services. So dressed in our Sunday best, Kathy and I would go with Dad to mass. I remember, just as we went out the door for church, mom would grab her worn white-covered Bible, a cup of coffee, and turn the little black and white console television to evangelist Oral Roberts or Billy Graham. Mom sat ready for her own shut- in Sunday message.

* * *

Mom had just had her August 1st birthday and turned 48 in 1989. I never really believed my mom would die. I thought she was too young. I was wrong.

Mom had been getting exceedingly fatigued and had been to the doctor eight months before for a congestive heart. Mom was on medicine and was doing OK, so when I got the call that she had been taken to the hospital, I was stunned.

At the hospital, the doctors pulled my dad, my sister, and me aside to discuss mom's condition. They told us that she was the sickest one on the entire floor. I asked the doctors, "Is she going to make it?" There was no response from her team of doctors who looked around at each other. The silence was the answer I did not expect. The doctors showed us an x-ray of her heart on a large lit box. Her heart looked much smaller than my fist and resembled a small piece of blackened charcoal on the film. "It's most likely from all the treatment that was administered during her cancer. We don't know how she even managed to live this long."

I knew how she managed to live. Mom's request to live and to let her raise her girls was an answered prayer. Now the doctors asked us what we wanted to do if things turned…bad. An option would be to place her on life support. When I asked if she could have a transplanted heart or some other treatment, they shook their heads slowly and said, "No, she is not a candidate for transplant since she had cancer." It turns out that damaged myocardium is not something people get transplants for.

The difficult question was open for our discussion. Could mom remain on life support indefinitely, especially if there were no medical treatments for her weak heart? Dad, Kathy, and I, looked sadly at each other. We knew the answer. Mom had suffered all her life.

We went into mom's hospital room to talk with her. I looked at her lying in bed awake and tears immediately filled my eyes. Mom peacefully asked, "What's wrong, honey?" I answered,

"Mom, the doctors say you're the sickest one on the floor and you're not going to make it." Mom looked into my frightened eyes, and nodded her head slowly up and down as if she already knew. "We love you so much," we said through flowing tears.

She calmed our fears of life without her as we all talked for a bit, and then we let her get some rest.

After hearing the grim news and seeing my mom's acceptance of her critical circumstances, I spent time praying in the hospital chapel. We needed a miracle.

In the chapel, I had a serious talk with God. I kneeled and pleaded through streaming tears. I selfishly told Him of all the people in mom's life that needed her here. I repented and told God I was sorry for all the stress I caused in my parents' life. I had recently divorced and had a little 3-year-old girl, who was the apple of grandma's eye. I wanted so much for my mom to live.

My father is a great dad, devoted spouse and integrity-filled Illinois State Trooper. What would happen to my dad without her? Kathy was finishing her graphic arts degree and away at college. She needed mom in her life too. I was reeling from my life thus far. I knew God already knew all this information, but I was urgently begging for a miracle if it was His will.

I openly sobbed loudly not caring who was in the chapel. I noticed there were a handful of others in the dimly lit room. Perhaps they were also praying for a miracle. One concerned and compassionate woman came over and leaned toward me and asked, "What's wrong, dear? Is there anything I can do?" Through tears, I looked at her and said, "My mom is dying." At about the same time, the creaky chapel door opened in the back and a panicked-looking nurse asked if Karen was in here. I needed to come quick.

Without caring what a commotion I would cause, I sprinted through the halls, screaming, pushing, and catching elevators.

Bursting into her room, I could see and hear blaring alarm bells and lots of flashing equipment indicating an emergency - a code. Nurses and doctors were running all around shouting instructions while Dad and Kathy stood at the end of her bed helplessly watching. I joined them there.

Mom was intubated, but she looked as though she were struggling for air, as she thrashed about. Watching her in misery, trying to get air was extremely heart wrenching.

Dad, Kathy, and I wanted mom to live, but in the end was it really our decision? Finally, after watching mom's great efforts to breathe, I could take it no more and painfully said, "Please, just let her go… DNR." Dad, Kathy, and I looked at each other and nodded in agreement. The doctors and nurses stopped what they were doing and all at once sympathetically stared at us.

Hearing the do not resuscitate, the medical team slowed their frantic pace and removed tubes and wires from mom. We moved in to comfort and hold our mom as she passed.

I was 23 and my little sister just 20 when Mom passed away on August 18, 1989, from heart failure. I guess God knew Kathy and I were not little girls anymore and wanted her home to be with Him. Time and again, I think of Mom asking to stay on earth to raise us, and how she was granted her desire. A messenger breeze, hospital visiting apparitions, I could see why she might have been apprehensive to tell us.

Perhaps she waited to tell us of her angelic encounters in hopes of protecting us from a rejecting world if we shared her unworldly experiences. What I most reminisce about when I think of my mother was how she listened attentively as we prayed at night before bed to our guardian angel.

I always felt my mom's unconditional love for us and saw her acceptance of others. Her quiet personality, her gentle caring spirit, and her gentleness of spirit were notable traits my sister Kathy also displayed throughout her short life.

I was reliving those last moments with my mother when I was jarred to the present - day reality.

It was after 2 a.m., and a body was being recovered from the icy water.

CHAPTER 5

Gathering Thoughts

For death is no more than a turning of us over from time to eternity *-William Penn*

Rescuers lined the bank of the levee and crowded around the divers at the cold water's edge to form a semi-circle. From my vantage point on the small hill, I peered around trees allowing myself to watch, then to look away when the scene grew too intense then, watch again, and then look away. The men's bulky gear as they hovered at the edge of the water, combined with the glaring lights made seeing who was recovered impossible.

My heart abruptly sank as it was becoming more of a certainty for me that my nephew, his friend, and my little sister may all be lying at the bottom of the murky lake awaiting recovery- their young lives lost.

I fled from my waterside post and voluntarily went into the house to see the family. Inside those gathered were mostly silent, quietly weeping. Seeing the families so devastated made me gasp in despair. Experiencing all the emotional weight of what was transpiring as they learned the news of a body recovered - was absolutely devastating. "How can I handle all this?" "I CAN'T." My emotional strength was exhausted. I returned outside.

Once more, I situated myself on the top of the driveway as close as the rescuers would allow. More than ever I wanted to scream in agony at the top of my lungs, and break through their human barricades. I knew I had to contain myself if I were going to be permitted to see my family.

Whenever my sister called upon me, for whatever the reason, being her sis, I would be there no matter what the situation, to give guidance or protection. Kathy and I had a strong and loving bond. It is a sacred connection that sisters intimately have for each other, or at least we did. We were close.

Now, I was experiencing so much extreme anxiety about losing that intimate bond that I could hardly slow down my rapid, shallow, now hyperventilating breaths. My head forceful throbbed to a pulsing beat. I was feeling absolutely defenseless and could do nothing to protect her now.

Kathy and I grew even closer, as we matured to adults, further strengthening our bond. I always felt like my mom was with me still when I was with my sister. "Would both my sister and my mom's memory become now lost to me?" I agonized. "

Kathy indeed had my mom's mannerisms- that gentle soul who was compassionate, a great listener, and inner and outer natural beauty, which others found striking. My sis looked most graceful, though, when she was riding on her horse. Her long, dark, naturally curly hair, as thick as her horse's mane, bounced in unison as she galloped around the arena when she was riding. I always thought how exceedingly stunning my sister was.

* * *

Pacing back and forth on the gravel driveway in full panic, I pleaded, "Where is God in all this?" I continued to fiercely pace, "WHERE ARE YOU?" I was given a reply to my posed question when my mind was abruptly filled with Bible scripture. I felt as though I was physically struck in the head- the awareness of the words was incredibly overpowering. Bits and pieces of verses ran through my mind with the sentences starting, stopping, and combining in a spliced together manner which I heard inside my head. It sounded as though hundreds of different voices, at different pitches, were rapidly speaking scripture at the same time with no particular comprehensible order. But I innately knew it was Bible verses which all combined to sound like a steady hum.

I remember plainly hearing Psalm 23, "Though I walk through the valley of the shadow of death"...then the sound of wordy garbled sentences. The buzzing words sounded as if they were playing on an old style tape player - with the tape ribbon being fast-forwarded. I felt the need to cover my ears with my hands to try and somehow slow the bounding words. The action did not lessen the bombardment. The entire Bible was fast-tracked inside my human brain and I was expected to process the divine verbiage to make sense of it. This was beyond human understanding.

Countless verses about suffering, hope, and love, streamed together in spiritual cadence.

"Are these barraging verses intended to be comforting to me at such a desperate time?"

If only I had the unshakable faith, at my darkest moment, to believe I was experiencing pure divinity. I wanted more…I so wanted something undeniably supernatural, like my mother experienced in her time of need, something unmistakably heavenly. I'm just human.

"I NEED MORE!"

Perchance, misty angelic apparitions to bring me comfort and a clear course was what I expected.

"Was my faith becoming quickly frozen." I held in my distress.

I was desperately seeking the Lord's comforting touch but felt alone. I felt frozen. These scrambled Bible verses reeling in my mind were obvious and intense. Was God trying to show me by filling my mind with His words that He was indeed with me?

* * *

The authorities came up to the house to inform us that the recovered body was my nephew's friend, Austin.

Then I saw before me a family destroyed. The rescuers needed a positive identification on the boy's body so off went a distressed father to identify his son. Escorted by others, he crossed onto the levee and out of my direct line of sight. When he returned and approached the house, he could not stand and walk on his own without assistance. His feet dangled as he was almost carried back shouldered by others once again up to the house to his awaiting wife. I saw the devastated look upon his face and my heart broke for him and his wife.

Kathy and Kadin had become close to this family. They had many things in common like their love of horses. Both had fearless boys the same age, enjoyed fitness and gym workouts, but an even greater love they all shared was religious values.

CHAPTER 6

Numbness

A person's days are determined;
you have decreed the number of his months
and have set limits he cannot exceed.

-Job 14:5

Divers returned to the water after recovering Austin, and I knew the next bodies to be discovered could possibly be Kathy and Kadin. I watched the water slowly churn again as the rubber boat edged its way back over the pond following the guide of the overhead rope.

When divers search and recover, they are in murky water with low visibility. I heard it described as being in a very dark room and feeling your way around, hoping to touch what you are looking for. This pond was around 12 to 18 feet deep, and there were submerged trees and branches, intended cover for fish, which could easily catch on their clothes, snagging them below.

As I waited on the hill for updates, suddenly I felt strongly compelled to go into the house to fetch a dry bath towel. I had absolutely no idea why I would need such a cloth? Still, it seemed almost instinctive to return with the downy-soft towel to the driveway. Slowly the minutes seemed to pass from the first recovery of Austin.

Then I saw an agent approach with a somber expression on his face. With family and dear friends at my side, I learned the divers had located another body.

I saw the words form across his lips of the messenger in what appeared to me to be deliberately delivered in slow motion.

"They found your sister."

Then the words registered…

I experienced bursts of radiant flashes of light. The brilliant eruption appeared to be in my mind and vision like thousands of camera flashes going off simultaneously. I squinted from the intensity of the bolts of brightness I was experiencing.

"I'm going to pass out!" I held.

"Oh, my God, help me."

"My sister is dead!"

"She's DEAD."

Terror filled me. My violently shaking legs buckled beneath me, and I was left supported by the tight hugs of loved ones. I sobbed and wailed uncontrollably in utter agony.

"Oh, my poor sister, Oh, my poor sister," I repeated loudly.

The white streaks of light continued to fly at and inside me in a violent rage doing viscous circles increasing in intensity. My eyes were rapidly blinking and my chest felt savagely ripped open and flooded fiercely out. My heart pounded and pleaded to burst -it begged to stop. I had an urgent, frantic need to see Kathy as soon as possible.

I *must* see my sister…

The rescuers would indeed allow me to see her. Even though they had repeatedly warned against it, I had somehow swayed them. I would be escorted to my sis after my brother-in-law positively identified her. My husband would also accompany him to the ambulance lending him emotional support.

They returned in silence. Through their tightly puckered lips and weeping eyes, I could feel them pleading for me not to have to see what they just did. I did not regret watching the recovery process and I would not regret seeing her now. No matter what she may look like?

I was escorted to the ambulance along with my husband and dad. I passed along the levee and saw faces of distraught firefighters with horror-stricken faces on my left side and the edge of deaths dark water on the right. I approached the ambulance and saw the stretcher inside with the covered body. I picked up speed and leaped into the ambulance where they slowly uncovered Kathy.

Then I saw my sister… my heart stopped.

I saw her lifeless on the stretcher and immediately felt her panicked struggle in the water rush through my entire body. I knelt down next to her inside the ambulance and hugged her hard trying to cover my body over her. I pressed my face against hers. My watery tears mixed with the water that was weeping from her body and briefly, I paused to hear or feel her breath from her nostrils.

Her perfect body was so very cold, so frozen. I took her hand and rubbed it deeply as if I could warm her to life. Her clothes clung tightly to her. They were completely saturated with the icy water. Her toes were covered only with thin white socks. Knowing my sister, she knew she was going into the water and wearing her boots could hamper her efforts to save so she left them at the levee where they were discovered. I was distressed that her vacant body did not look at all at peace. It was evident she had physically struggled before passing from this life.

I took the plush towel I'd brought down from the house and tried to dry her water-soaked body and feet. Her toes felt so frozen, immovable as my fingers passed over each one of them. I wrapped her feet with the thick towel using it as makeshift pair of slippers. Oh, how I wanted to warm her feet as if to make her comfortable. Kathy strongly disliked feeling chilly from cold weather, and she disliked winter. Knowing my sister, she would want her feet to stop being cold.

As kids, Kathy and I played in snowdrifts, enjoyed sledding down the hill of our front yard, and rolling snow for snowball fights or snowmen. But the cold of winter was not something we enjoyed so much as adults. We much preferred the warmth of summer.

I have such fond childhood memories of the summertime. Family vacations included lying on a beach, digging sand trenches with my little sister, all the while our family basked in the glory of the sun. We regularly ventured to Panama City

Beach in Florida, which seemed to be my parents' favorite drive to getaway. Florida sun always felt intense, so much warmer to me than Illinois sun. Unfortunately, the warming sunrays usually burned my fairer skin while Kathy's skin was incredibly tolerant and it would not take much for her skin tone to deepen to a beautiful brown.

Staring at Kathy lying lifeless on the stretcher, her body did not have a radiant glow from a sunny day now. With my fingertips I traced along her face several times against the wishes of the authorities. "Please don't touch her," they requested of me. The command did not at all register because I did not care at that moment if I interfered with any investigative procedures, if that was of concern. I repeated over and over, "My poor beautiful sister."

My only sibling, my kid sister, was lying on a gurney… dead.

Cold water drained slowly from Kathy's ears and a watery fleshy-pink gash was on her right cheek. Her finger nails were damaged, and she had wounds on exposed skin.

I saw her great effort to live in her body injuries and deep in the still of her open blue eyes. I knew Kathy's eyes were now fixed upon Paradise. I reached to try to close her eyelids, seeing them open for the last time. I did not want to leave her side.

I looked up from Kathy at my heartbroken dad. Here we were again experiencing unimaginable loss in our family.

We exiting the ambulance and began our walk back up the hill to the house. This time I paused to look at the rescuers and exchange traumatized glances. This was hard on them, too.

Re-entering my sister's house, I headed straight to her bedroom as if being drawn there. I realized I had just seen my sister lying lifeless in the ambulance. I fell hard to my knees, collapsing by her side of the bed. I wailed uncontrollably into her thick covers, grasping at the blankets and her horse-printed pillowcases. I was frantically weeping, panting and could not catch my breath. I could not breathe in our exhale a full breath, but then again I did not really want to breathe.

I wanted to die. I wrapped my arms tightly around myself and rocked back and forth as if to bring comfort to my body. I drove my head deep into the bed cover and began quietly speaking and singing disjointed words and verses through my agony. I recollect incomprehensibly trying to sing and cry simultaneously to a Casting Crowns song, *Praise You in This Storm,* all while semi-lifting my hand as if in a trance-like state of worship. What was I even doing?

How could I possibly be in a position to praise at a time like this? Through blurry tear-filled eyes, I looked to my right and become aware of my pastor alongside the bed now kneeling, consoling, and praying with me. The earthly life of my sister and nephew had done a complete circle. My pastor was there when Kathy accepted Christ and Kadin grew to know Christ and now he was here as they ended their walk on earth.

As sisters do, we confided in each other about so many things. I recalled a time when Kathy and I had questions about our faith and shared with each other how we seldom felt encouraged from the time we spent in church. Kathy and I wondered if we would ever be good enough to make it into heaven. We desired some assurance we were on the right path, even though we knew we were reasonably good girls. Maybe God would look at our lives and see we did do things for Him and others. We memorized prayers and we prayed before we ate meals.

Kathy and I knew there was no way we wanted to be left behind and not make it to be evaluated at Heaven's gates. We knew our mom was there in Paradise, along with other family, and our souls longed very much to be with them and our creator God.

One "gets out" of a religious service I believe what one puts into it. Church is not about being entertained. Many people thrive in churches just like the one we grew up in. However, at this point in our lives, we were still searching… I never really considered church "shopping" before.

"Wouldn't that be a sin?" I wondered.

Still, we both felt a stirring, a thirst inside, a want to find more in this life, learn more, and offer ourselves more, especially in the area of faith and religion.

We both had a deep calling, a true desire to be sold out for Jesus. We just needed to find such a place to grow with others who wanted to also be sold out. We needed to become un-stagnated. So, 2002 became a year of new religious beginnings, a renewal, for Kathy and me as we searched.

There was a non-denominational church, which had a modest building, but always had inspirational verses placed on a lighted marquee next to a busy highway. I often reflected on those inspiring and rousing words on my daily drive to and from work.

"What kind of a church has plain vinyl siding?" or "a chat rock parking lot?" no church I had ever gone into that was for sure. "Where was the enormous steeple and stained glass?" Even with all these cosmetic concerns, I wanted to find out more about the roadside church and told my sister my thoughts. I did not actually contemplate making a church change up until this point. The choice was really about choosing everlasting life, not about the church construct.

One Sunday morning in the summer, I decided to get my courage up and see what this "Hope" non-denominational church was about. I had not been in a church with such an optimistic adjective for a name before. I had so many religious questions and I sought answers. Would I find some answers at a place called hope? I did not know- but was hoping the answers would come.

So, here I was parked in front of church on the gravel lot (for quite some time) with my 18-year- old daughter, Danielle. I was hesitating and deciding if we should enter the framed building. My daughter, however, had a much different perspective on this church and tried to reassure me and explain that it would be OK but different for me. My ex-husband had, for some time, been going to a non-denominational church so on the weekends my daughter was with him when she was younger, she attended his church. I alleged in the beginning he was taking her to some sort of cult and panicked. My ex and I had talked about the Bible at that time, and he put my fears to rest. He told me about charismatic Catholics, and he convinced me that I was just being rash and in a true sense prejudice.

Various ideas ran through my mind as we sat outside waiting. "Maybe the people inside are so-called Jesus freaks like I've seen in movies"? "Then again, what is a Jesus freak?" I wondered. Might going through those doors really be a sin I am knowingly thinking of committing? After all, I had only been a member of one church my entire life.

My mother, on the other hand, grew up going to and experiencing a variety of churches. She told me stories of when she was a girl, on any given Sunday she would go to different denominational services with her friends. Perhaps I was envisioning this church service at Hope being like one my mom often told Kathy and me as a bedtime story.

She told us during service at one church the congregation would leave their seats and roll all over the aisle on the ground. Mom called this a Holy Roller church. I asked mom, "What would make the people want to get their nice church clothes wrinkled and dirty?" My mom chuckled.

Risking the possibility I would one day burn in hell for going through the door of this church with my daughter alongside me, we went cautiously to the worship service. I didn't recognize anyone, except the pastor and his family so I knew I was safe with this "church shopping" secret. I was worried, though, about what my family would think when they found out.

That first service, while seated in my gray metal folding chair, stirred a spiritual revival to begin inside me. I didn't recognize any of the songs during the service, yet I really enjoyed the fast tempo with instruments that I had never heard before in church. The song lyrics were projected on a large screen above the musicians so all could see them and follow along. I recall thinking how many songs they sang, far more than I had expected. The songs were so upbeat I could have kept listening to more even after the music set ended.

There were no familiar missalettes to read and follow along with, but everyone had a Bible they held and gladly opened to read. People would clap and feel so moved they put their arms up during the service. I even heard people saying "Amen" even when no one else said it. No one repeated prayers, daydreamed, or looked at their watch. The service was definitely much longer than I was used to, but I wanted it to keep going and not stop. I sat and cried softly to myself thinking how moving this church experience made me feel.

The pastor asked if anyone needed to accept Christ. I watched intently as men and women went up to the front of church and asked for prayer. The thought of actually making a choice to follow Christ was intriguing - following Him was a choice, "A choice?" I could freely make a decision on my own without going through someone else to say necessary prayers for me. I felt freedom here to worship God in a completely new way - a very personal way.

"WOW, look what I found!" I left the service thinking. I wanted to tell my family what freshness I felt so I talked with my sister first. She was excited, because I was so energized by the experience. Kathy wanted to learn more and I told her everything I knew.

Kathy's older son Keegan and my son are not even a year apart in age, and we wanted them to grow up in a thriving church environment. Our mom and dad brought religion into our lives, and we wanted to instill Jesus into our families as well.

The next Sunday came and my sister and I, together with my daughter and our boys, went to church together. Our kids thoroughly enjoyed the age-specific programs. They made new friends, and even memorized scripture verses willingly. The churchgoers were all so genuine and very easy to get to know. Soon, my husband started to attend the services and some of my sister Kathy's in- laws began coming as well.

Kathy and I attended Bible studies and quickly grew in our renewed Christian faith. We found life in Christ here, and we both eagerly accepted Him and followed through with full-immersion Baptism. I reflected about how she was baptized into Christ with water and now she was with Christ after losing her life in water.

* * *

Feeling a considerable physical drain after giving up so much emotion and praying in my sister's bedroom, my mind slowed momentarily to fully focus on the unanswered question, "Where is my nephew?"

CHAPTER 7

Kadin turns Se7en

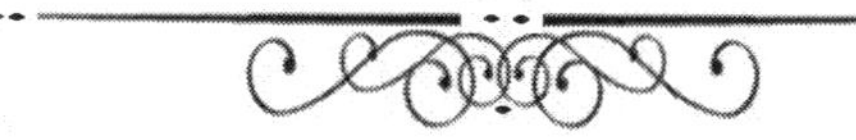

The day which we fear as our last is but the birthday of eternity. -Seneca / philosopher

As before, I buried my face down into the thick covers of my sister's bed. I was thinking fondly about Kadin.

"What does he want for his birthday?" I called and asked my sister a week before Kadin's big 7th birthday. She gave me a list of gift possibilities most of which centered on the Star Wars theme. In years past, he had requested toys like animated dinosaurs, monster or construction trucks, trains, or motorcycles. With a list of ideas, I went in search of Star Wars storm troopers, droid action figures, and a Millennium Falcon space ship.

The action figures were a good choice because I knew Kadin loved toys that had lots of moving parts. Equally though, he enjoyed playing with simple green Army men. He would strategically line the little army up so the plastic men were ready to attack the foe when the alarm sounded to advance the troops. One thing is for sure -my nephew loved action.

With the Star Wars toys I planned to gift him on his birthday, I knew he could load up the Millennium spaceship and imagine flying in space shooting lasers at the enemy. He already had a wide assortment of Star Wars figures so this would add to his collection. This gift, I predicted, would provide hours of entertainment for Kadin. His presents, all wrapped in sports-themed paper, had all the high-energy activities he enjoyed doing.

I knew Kadin was going to the movies Friday night to celebrate his 7th birthday and that he had invited a friend along for the fun. I decided to give the gifts early to him on the night before his birthday knowing we may not be able to see him until after his big day. While Kadin was at his brother's baseball training, we watched him open his surprises.

Kadin was well pleased. "Aw, this is what I wanted!" he said loudly. It was wonderful to see my nephew enjoy his birthday gifts and see his huge smile.

* * *

Kadin had little fear when it came to trying daring activities especially when he supposed the possibly dangerous feat might end up being fun. Kadin thought his young age did not matter and that he could instantly try the things his older brother could do. His brother Keegan did stunts using all types of wheels like dirt bikes, four wheelers, and skateboards. Kadin enjoyed those as well and loved jumping off his hard plastic ramp outside on the sidewalk with his Spiderman folding scooter. Early on, it became apparent to me that Kathy's boys had inherited a dose of their mom's fun-loving gutsiness.

Kadin was much like my sister at that age. Kathy was fearless on her bike and skateboards also, and loved to maneuverer around and over obstacles. She admired motorcyclist Evel Knievel and had a dare devil stunt action play set. She could pose the Evel Knievel action figure, move his arms and legs on the motorcycle and launch the cycle through simulated rings of fire.

My sister was the tomboy-type of girl who mostly disliked dressing up in frilly dresses unless it was mandatory. She much preferred her hair in twisted braids and wearing pants with tennis shoes. This worked well during playtime because she, just like Kadin, used to play hard and get dirty. I knew all along my little sis was married she could not wait to have boys of her own to roughhouse with. Kathy was undeniably overjoyed when she was blessed with her first son, and then another.

On the football field, even at Kadin's young age, he made some awesome tackles. My nephew was so solidly built he was unafraid to take down anybody. He also played baseball, hitting off a tee, and loved when he got a hit. He had a precious grin so wide one could not help but smile back. My mind was intently wrapping around how tragic that on Kadin's 7th birthday, a day that is supposed to bring joy that they had all perished? There was no joy now ...no smiling.

* * *

I lifted off Kathy's bedside and headed back outside to see the efforts to recover Kadin. The team of fatigued rescuers was searching the frigid water for hours. We learned the diver's tanks were almost out of air. They were deciding if it was even feasible to try recovering Kadin in what was left of the night. Their thinking was that at dawn, when the sun rose, it would be more practical. Sometime had passed since Kathy's recovery, I could not endure thinking little Kadin was at the bottom of the dark, cold pond alone. The image was heart wrenching.

In my desperation, I pleaded, "Please, find my nephew. Don't leave him in the dark water alone." Even though the divers had spent hours already in the dark icy water, they kept up the search awhile longer. The dive team was extraordinary and courageous.

Then the word came - the divers had recovered Kadin. No one had survived. My sister Kathy, my nephew Kadin, and his friend had all died a watery death.

* * *

It was now somewhere between 4a.m. and sunrise-the time of the day I most despise. My mother died during this time, and I know the hauntingly bleak hours all too well.

There was a slow retreat from the surreal scene. First ambulances, minus red emergency lights, carried our loved ones away to undergo autopsies since they were unattended deaths. Fire trucks and vehicles full of weary rescuers withdrew next. The police, however, stayed awhile longer. - posted on the long driveway to assist in giving our families protected privacy.

I found myself not wanting to go home. I could not retreat. More than anything, I felt their presence when they were alive here a few hours before. Around the inside of the house, birthday balloons and decorations were hanging in celebration of Kadin turning 7.

There was no celebrating now…

The family was shattered and completely exhausted. My brother-in-law and my now - awake nephew went to rest awhile in the master bedroom together. My brother-in-law without a wife and son and my poor nephew Keegan, recently turned 12, was now without his only brother and mom.

I was so saddened to think my sister would miss my nephew's major life events, graduations, driving, girlfriends, getting married, and grandkids - just maturing and growing up. My sister was such a wonderful wife and mother; she would be here for them in spirit without a doubt.

Although it was very early in the morning, the breaking news of three lives lost was filtering throughout the media community and broadcast beyond. Learning of the tragedy, church friends arrived at my sister's house and came to our side.

I prayed next to the pond with them forming a circle, supporting me to help me stay upright. I do not recall what was voiced, but I do remember feeling some comfort by the prayers. I could not turn my eyes from the sheen reflecting off the melting ice. Its mirrored surface shined intensely. With eyes partially closed in prayer, I was disrespectfully disturbed by a helicopter hovering overhead and obvious rustling noises from inquisitive reporters in the nearby fields disturbing underbrush.

So it began. The media had an ugly story to report and they wanted graphic pictures. My husband parked his truck blocking the drive, not allowing the reporters access up the mile driveway to seek out our family. When the relentless reporters, could not come via the rock road, they intended to find alternate routes through the open fields.

Quivering in anger, I turned and bellowed at the top of my lungs directly up into the air, "Just GO AWAY! Leave us alone." I would not have our family subjected to the media. I always wondered how anyone could go onto the news the same day of a tragedy and keep it together after losing loved ones. They appear so heartless while being media exploited.

The day was a blur- filled with countless phone calls.

Later into the night, my husband and I rested for a bit in Kadin's room with his dim light peeking from inside the closed closet door. Glancing around his construction-themed room in despair, I stopped at his toy chest. My dad had woodworked Kadin a large toy chest for his 1st birthday and atop it rested the birthday present we had given him earlier. The Star Wars Millennium Falcon was fully assembled and ready to be played with. Cardboard and plastic wrapping lay about and I could just imagine Kadin eager to begin playtime. He had added the storm trooper and droids to his collection of toys and had them arranged as if they were preparing to go on a new space mission.

After surveying the room with a sigh, I finally put my head down, burying it deep into my nephew's pillow. How I wished I could give Kadin a hug. I tucked my arm underneath to hold the pillow tighter. When I did, I discovered a hidden food treasure placed by Kadin. The prize was a bright orange Cheetos. The corn curl was a saved nighttime snack from his pillow stash, I imagine. The idea of Kadin and his secret stockpile made me smile and cry at the same time.

CHAPTER 8
Moments to Mourn

When I heard these things, I sat down and wept. For some days I mourned and fasted and prayed before The God of heaven.

-Nehemiah 1:3-5

I fell into a light sleep on Kadin's bed. All too soon, though, I fully awoke after what I had hoped was just a horrific dream and not true.

But it was true - they were gone. The sun did rise that day, but the world was silent. This was surely a morning to mourn…

I was the only one stirring, so I wandered quietly around my sister's house looking at everything anew. The home smelled of woodsy jasmine and lavender. I soaked in the scent as I fully appreciated every feminine, motherly touch my sister brought to the home. I paused near the kitchen and whispered out their names.

"Kathy, are you here? Kadin…"

How I desperately wanted them both to say they were still with us.

Yet, spoken using a soft voice their beautiful names choked in my throat, which felt parched and constricted. Squinting through swollen eyes, I imagined them casually standing in the kitchen as if it were a typical morning. Both would be wearing warm pajamas on this cold winter morning, and my sister would be enjoying a sip from her hot cup of flavored coffee. My nephew would be drinking juice at the counter waiting for his breakfast.

Grabbing a few inflated birthday balloons from the kitchen, I wandered outside to see the sun gently waking almost winking from the horizon as it began its rise over the underbrush of twigs and trees. The sunshine ushered in the light of a new day to reveal the entrenched aftermath on the levee of the horrifying and unforgettable nighttime scene.

I could hear only the pining whinnies of horses, breaking the quietude. Motionless, I turned to face the barn, mentally picturing my early-rising sister walking to the stable to give the horses their scheduled morning feed. The horses would have to wait.

Faintheartedly I ambled down the gravel road to the pond. Did I really want to go there? I proceeded down the entrenched tire marks in the driveway that showed all the deep divots from the rescue vehicles and followed the path they made to the water's edge. I gazed upon the dark water that was now still and almost tranquil but eerie. Was this now-serene spot *really* the terror-filled scene of death? "Yes… it certainly was."

I stood shaking by the pond and focused on the spot where they might have fell through into the icy water. I played horrific, frenzied scenes in my head and imagined seeing little arms reaching skyward from the water. Were there panicked screams or was it …silent.

Then I realized something as I lingered there - the ice covering the pond was melting away. "The ice is melting!" When I first recognized the fact the ice was melting, I felt gripping knife-edged pain in my stomach that felt like my body was deeply slashed in half. I doubled over because I knew if this tragic accident had happened today, they might still be alive as there would have been no ice to complicate a rescue. "How could this have happened?" I was numb as uncontrollable chills ran up and down my body. I had to sit down.

I imagined the unimaginable. As I sat still I began hearing their fright-filled voices in what was now just the ongoing silence of wintertime. I envisioned over and over all the scenarios that could have ended their young lives.

As was typical, Kathy undoubtedly saw to the stables, tending to the horses making sure they had their evening feedstuff. She took such good care of those animals, making sure the stable was well kept. Kathy would have been wearing her name-brand stable attire by Arriat, bulky mud boots, and rugged gloves to get the job accomplished. She would take her thick, dark hair, braid it back, and throw on a cap. Though s my sister was slim, it never ceased to amaze me how she would happily shovel horse dung and toss a hay bale with passion. Kathy always had a contented glow about her, even in the manure.

Kathy would be finishing caring for the horses and gathering up belongings to prepare to drive Kadin and Austin to the movie. The boys would be playing about carefree, excited to be leaving soon. It is especially hard for me to imagine just the moment when my sister came to the dreadful realization she would jump into the water to rescue. As a mother, I trust she knew what must be done, but she was heroically brave to do it.

She would have had no time to think, only time to react on her gut instincts. I could see her violently shedding clothing articles, which she knew may weigh her down once in the water. Hence, the trail of her boots and gloves left along the levee. She was running full speed on coursing adrenaline, onto the frozen pond. The thin ice, unable to handle any weight whatsoever, gave way below her feet as she tried desperately to reach the center of the pond. I can't go on…

* * *

I raised my tired body up from the levee and bent over the water. I saw my glassy, watery reflection and imagined their faces looking tenderly back at me. Atop the pond I thoughtfully placed the balloons. Three birthday balloons - red, yellow, and blue - floated onto the melting pond to represent Kathy, Kadin, and Austin. I whispered,

"Happy Birthday, Kadin".

I watched the colorful balloons stay mystifyingly close together and peacefully float directly over to the place where the ice had broken. "Was this marker the exact spot that claimed their lives?"

I imagined the air-filled balloons filled with their last breaths…

Heavy tears welled once more in the corners of my strained eyes and streamed down my cheeks as I fixated on the three balloons. Over and over again, I replayed the boys' and my sister's efforts to fight to stay alive. I screamed aloud, "God, where are you in all this? ...WHERE?"

* * *

There was something compelling about the water. I found it difficult to leave the spot of their deaths. Perhaps if I stayed put, they would return by some miracle. Maybe they were all hovering near and would give me an unmistakable sign. Then a Bible story came to mind. After Jesus died and was laid in the tomb, his followers came to find him lying dead, but He had risen. He was not there. Even though I wanted so badly to feel them all near, they were not here.

For me, leaving here was an acceptance of their deaths, and I just could not go there...

It was time, though, to go home for some rest before preparing funeral arrangements in the afternoon. Two nights had passed with very little sleep, yet my sleep-deprived body endured. Understandably, my brother-in- law said he had never talked about this sort of thing, funeral planning with Kathy, and that I might know better about what she may want. I assured him I would help make their memorial service one that would honor them. I hugged my brother–in-law and my nephew before leaving. They needed time to be alone.

Leaving the house required driving over the levee. I thought about how my nephew and brother-in-law would have a constant reminder of their enormous loss every time they went on the driveway and saw the water. As our car passed slowly over the levee, I could not take my focus off the spot in the now- melting pond where the ice opening claimed their lives just hours earlier. The three birthday balloons I placed on the water's edge remained floating together and fixed where the ice gave way and the three perished.

I was utterly exhausted both mentally and physically. Once at home, I began to feel my body's pain. I took a hot shower and noticed long scrapes, deep gashes from thicket branches and thorny underbrush that I had gone into during my frantic search for them. Some of the cuts were stinging and some had already crusted from the blood that ran from the cuts. I noticed several tender-to-the-touch areas on my arms and legs, which I supposed were bruises in the making. My body knew how to repair itself by forming a scab. How would my body heal itself from a broken heart?

The bed would feel good yet the idea of just dozing off to sleep was not a real possibility. My mind was full of horrid images as I restlessly lay my head on the pillow. Then I recollected what I was at home doing at the exact time when the three of them had their lives cut short. I was in the other room doing a painting on canvas.

Painting has been a lifelong hobby of mine. Acrylic paint is my medium of choice because it dries more rapidly than oils and works well with the creative techniques I enjoy. Acrylics also give me a quick creative outlet, since I am an emotion-driven artist and paint abstract images. While I continued to try to rest my eyes, I thought about the *repulsive* picture I painted the night before.

When I began painting that evening, I intended to create an original painting for friends as a gift for their upcoming wedding that I would be attending. After seeing what was creatively unfolding on the canvas through the paint I applied, I was sure that I would not be giving this work to anyone as a wedding gift.

It was dreadful. This painting was turning out to be one that I knew I needed to take a fully loaded paintbrush of white paint to, and smear all over the canvas to start anew. On the canvas lay mainly shades of black with gold. While I was painting, I recognized the fact that I rarely paint with gold paint. Be that as it may, I felt the need to continue to focus on applying the metallic gold copiously. A sculptured grey boney hand rested cupped open on the lower half of the canvas while white slapdash streaks ran along the top. In truth, I strongly disliked how this painting was developing but I continued painting even though it disgusted me. Eyeing its black runny paint mingling with the radiant gold made me nauseous and I shook my head, repulsed, and said aloud, "This is the ugliest painting I have ever painted!" I continued to feel nauseous and stopped painting briefly, so I could go vomit. I assumed the paint smell must have got the best of me or I ate something that disagreed and I was becoming sick. In all honesty I was *physically* ill over creating this hideous painting.

I stopped and called a friend to tell her I had just become sick over painting my most revolting work ever. She assured me, in her kind fashion, it was probably not as bad as I dramatized, but I truly knew it was a dark appalling painting. Even though the painting personally disgusted me, I would let the colors dry and mull over it later.

After the nausea from analyzing the ugly painting passed, I found myself surprisingly inspired. I heard a clear voice in my mind say, "Now, go, and paint something happy." I thoroughly washed the black and gold acrylic paint caked on the long handled brushes. The rinse water blackened to a murky dark shade with the dissolving gold specks shimmering and floating mostly atop the water.

When I begin a painting, I usually try to finish it in one extended artistic session. This style works for me because I am compelled to complete the project quickly, letting my emotions fill the work. For this reason, I find it difficult to stop my creative process and put the brush down once I start, fearing I might miss the moment of a canvas masterpiece.

The new canvas once coated in a mix of acrylic paints, brought a less bleak palette than the first painting that evening.

Brushstrokes of yellow goldenrod-brown, buttercreams, and earth tones layered the canvas. I chalked an abstract face of Christ on the right side of the painting while the canvas was in the drying stage. Three white crosses began taking shape on the left side, so I went with the forms and continued using the pure white pastel palette. I was satisfied with the "happier" painting. I was tired so I decided to apply any needed details to the work once the paint fully dried by morning.

* * *

As I lay on my bed unable to stop the torrent of thoughts, I realized I was creating that unpleasant dark painting when they were dying! While the three of them were fading from this life, drowning in the freezing water, I was painting the tragedy as it happened. "Was I being inspired to paint their last moments on canvas?" If that were indeed the case, had I captured in my painting …*death*?

Might this dark canvas of disgust, represent my sister Kathy, Kadin, and Austin's deaths? An overflow of powerful emotions gave me chills as I wondered if it were really true.

Curious, I got up out of bed and was eerily drawn to the dark painting. As soon as I looked at the painting again, it instantly made me shudder…and I knew in my heart the truth. When I had sat down the previous night, I had no way of knowing what was occurring during the hours I was painting. It was difficult looking at the looming picture still; I studied each brushstroke, and tried desperately to make sense of the ominous images.

The title of the painting would be *At the Time of Death*.

Recalling last evening, after I had finished talking to my friend about the now not-so-appealing painting, I heard a commanding, familiar voice in my head saying, "Now, go and paint something happy!" At the time, I had actually snickered and thought, "That comment is so something Kathy would be saying to me."

My sister often said my paintings had such dark undertones. I constantly looked to her to be my constructive criticizer believing her guidance. "Why don't you lighten that area there, or switch that color around or choose a shade brighter!"

Kathy completed her college degree in graphic design shortly after our mother passed away, and I was very proud of her determined accomplishment. Kathy was very apt to give me her artistic insight and as a general rule, I listened to her instruction. I had taken a few junior college art classes' decades ago but never finished an art degree. My sister tried to tutor me on the use of computers to creatively design, but for me using a keyboard and a mouse just weren't as satisfying as getting paint all over my hands. Now, without my sister's honesty as my personal art critic, I would be extra anxious about painting again without her feedback.

Just three months earlier, I had persuaded my sister into designing an art website so we could feature our artistic creations. We squabbled about what we should call our venture and opted to go with my sister's clever idea - lead2paint. Lead as in pencil or lead as to be divinely led to paint. The number two represented us- two sisters. We tossed ideas back and forth until we came up with just the right font and image for our unique motif. My sister was especially talented at designing logos, so the decision to use her attention-grabbing rendering was unanimous.

A talented friend, Julie, who enjoyed photography, offered to take pictures of Kathy and me together so we could put them on our sister site. Kathy was so naturally photogenic, but I generally disliked being photographed. The photos were first-rate and we had an amusing time during our photo session together. Once we had pieced the website together to both our liking, we launched the site lead2paint.com in January 2010. The site was not designed primarily to make money but to be a place for us to display our talents and testimonies as artists and sisters.

Kathy background was in the graphics field and she enjoyed design, toy packaging, and advertising layout. She unfortunately was soured by egotistical employers early on who did not much care for working with talented women. As a result, Kathy chose to be her own boss and do freelance work, which worked out well as she started her family. On occasion, she would also paint wall murals and stencil in people's homes.

I asked Kathy to consider moving her talents to a canvas, knowing that would be a change for her. Although she would not be creating on a wall or a computer, I believed she would embrace holding a brush and paper anew. I told her to consider our website as an added creative outlet. Since my sister's technique was expressing more in real-life, it took her far more time to complete her art than I. Because of her attention to detail, she only had one recent painting on canvas completed, that of her beloved horse. With every intention of continuing to pick up paintbrushes and embrace further canvas painting, her husband started constructing a proper art studio, above their garage, to give her space to create original works.

* * *

I returned once again to the bed that did not provide me any rest and continued to think about Kathy, Kadin, and the two paintings. I realized it was just 12 short hours ago when I rested the paintbrush. Unthinkable tragedy had occurred since I painted the two conflicting paintings. Now, I was lying in bed exhausted and in horrified shock over the magnitude of my family's loss.

With my thoughts briefly quieted, I could hold my pleading eyes open no longer and granted my body a mid-morning doze.

CHAPTER 9

Painful Planning

There are also heavenly bodies and there are earthly bodies; but the splendor of the heavenly bodies is one kind, and the splendor of the earthly bodies is another.
-1 Corinthians 15:39-41

Discussions centered on death and pre-arranging funeral requests are not generally an everyday dialog among most families. This does not come as a surprise to me as death, funeral preferences, and memorial services typically do not make for bubbly conversation.

Still, being very close to my sister, I felt I knew what her funeral wishes might be. First, Kathy would not want any attention focused on herself even in death. But then again, since I believe funerals are for the living, the ones left behind who have to grieve, I wanted Kathy and Kadin's short lives on earth to be celebrated.

I had been in this funeral-planning position before, for my mother and grandmother. Making choices becomes emotionally intense, so I reflected on what Kathy and Kadin would have selected just as if they were standing by my side telling me what they preferred. If you focus on what your loved one truly liked and appreciated on earth, it makes planning tolerable.

Some years ago, I was asked by a dear friend's father to help him complete a wish he had for his own pre-planned funeral. His aim was to have everything arranged ahead of time and have his own requests and items ready and waiting at the funeral home when his time came, making planning easier on his family. He asked me if I would paint a custom fabric casket covering to drape over the coffin during the wake. I agreed to paint the covering, but I had never painted such an offbeat request before.

He very much enjoyed wild mushroom hunting in the woods so he wanted a spring scene with sprouting morels and a saying that read, "I have enjoyed my stay on Earth," lettered on the casket cover. I painted his request on white silky fabric with blooming red bud trees. He also enjoyed making homemade wine and he told me he would also be holding a bottle of his libation as he rested in peace. To my knowledge at the time, he was not ill or dying. But since his passing, I understand his good judgment in taking some stress off his saddened relatives.

After completing the painted casket covering, I contemplated what I might want for my own funeral. Perhaps some Irish and Bluegrass songs featuring an upbeat violin, pine greenery mixed with pink and champagne colored roses set about the place, and a palm tree. Since Kathy and Kadin could not express their heartfelt wishes, I considered what my sister might have wanted for herself and her son.

I did have a few wishes of my own for Kathy and Kadin's funeral, which I hoped were in agreement with my bother- in-law's wants. My main wish was to keep my sister and my nephew together, literally.

"Can we bury them both in the same coffin?" I asked the funeral directors.

I quickly gathered this was not a common request. The funeral directors said they had only done it before for a mother and a stillbirth, but they would do some measurements and see if it could be done. I knew if Kathy had not gotten to Kadin as they were dying, she would want to have her son close to her now.

"Don't they make coffins for bigger people?" I inquisitively asked. They said there were larger coffins, but the selection was limited to just one type. The coffin was only available in a steel blue color. This was perfect because blue was their favorite.

My next request was to be allowed to prepare my sister and nephew by styling their hair and applying the make-up.

The morticians at the funeral home do remarkable transformations on corpses, but I felt called to do Kathy and Kadin's make-up and hair myself. Many have asked how I would ever want to do such a thing. I knew how they looked in life, and to me it was the final gift I could give them on earth. My artistic gifts would be used on the most beautiful canvases God had ever made. Besides this would not be the first time I had done makeup and hair for deceased loved ones.

There is a tremendous amount of unexplainable emotion associated with grief. Though I was in horrified shock over my mother's death, I managed to channel my sadness and styled her hair and applied her make-up when she passed away. I sincerely believed my mom would be unhappy if her foundation was too pale for her complexion or her hair was not styled as she normally liked wearing it. I knew exactly how Mom put up her hair in pins and put on her make-up. Over the years, I had watched and learned her cosmetic application techniques. Who better than I to apply it?

Kathy and I often played with our mother's cosmetics as kids. In the 1970s, Mom belonged to the mail order World of Beauty-Butterfly Group, These kits showcased eyeshades, perfumes, and foundations, to nail polish and were selected for my mom's choice of color palette. The beautifying kits arrived cushioned in Styrofoam bi-monthly to its members. Mom enjoyed discovering what was in the offering. Let's just say Kathy and I had plenty of make-up around the house to do beauty experiments on each other. This love of cosmetics continued through my adulthood as I am a Mary Kay beauty consultant.

My mom had faultless facial features, and I believe she wore cosmetics purely to enhance her natural beauty. She preferred the blue shades of eye shadow colors and her favorite lipsticks were pink tints. Mom went to lengths to look spectacular at all times. Because of her love of facial color, I knew mom would frown on neutral natural colors generally applied to people during funeral viewings. Mom would have said that they would wash out her darker completion.

People have also asked how I could touch my family when they are "like that." Preparing a body for burial is not a typical way for some to begin grieving. It did, however, feel right and comfortable for me to prepare their bodies for burial by making them look how they looked when they were alive. The experience was not in any way morbid for me. I did not believe they were in their bodies anyway but that their bodies were just a shell to hold their souls while they were on earth.

* * *

I gathered some of Kathy's make-up from her house along with clothes and jewelry and her small personal Bible to take to the funeral home. For my nephew, I asked his big brother Keegan to help me pick something out for him to wear. We talked a bit and then went into Kadin's closet. "He likes to wear his pajamas under his pants," my nephew said. "Then we will make sure he is wearing his pajamas, won't we!" So, we picked out some comfortable jammy pants with construction equipment designs on them. We also chose a pair of just- played-in, well- worn jeans picked up off the closet floor for Kadin to wear over them.

Kadin liked to layer clothes so we put a t-shirt under a striped button- down shirt to complete his look.

I asked my nephew what he thought his brother would like to take with him. We collected a Pokémon card, a green plastic soldier, and the blue tattered teddy bear he loved so much. The blue teddy was a gift from the hospital when Kadin was born. He kept that bear close at all times.

Several times, Kadin had mistakenly left his blue bear at different places, including my home. Kathy had to make a special trip to retrieve the bear for Kadin or his sleep time just would not be the same without his plush friend.

We received a phone call from the funeral home directors stating there was a matter of importance that they needed to clarify with a family member, so I volunteered since I was returning to the funeral home to deliver the clothing items. My sister and nephew's bodies had arrived, but the funeral home realized the boy's body may not actually be my nephew.

Upon entering the room, I focused on the white draped sheet. I quickly realized it was not Kadin, but his friend lying covered by the little sheet. He looked so peaceful, with powdery-smooth skin, - as though he was just napping. I thought to myself how glorious it would be to see Kadin and Austin, just two buddies, at play again.

The boys' bodies had been somehow switched, and Kadin's friend was to be cremated at another funeral home.

The mix up started the night they died. Since Kadin had been recovered after the other two, he was in a separate ambulance and Kathy and Austin were escorted in the first ambulance. The observant funeral directors promptly made the exchange to correct the matter before any final preparations had gotten underway.

* * *

After the switch, the funeral home called and said it was time to prepare Kathy and Kadin for the viewing. I readied myself and had a good friend, who was there when the bodies were recovered from the water, offered to come with me to the funeral home. I would not turn down the suggestion because I was truly a friend in need and welcomed the support while I prepared Kathy and Kadin. I knew what I was going to do, I'd done it before, but I knew he did not fully know what he had volunteered. That was fine because I could really use the kind-heartedness he offered.

We walked into the prep room which was lined in walls of stainless cabinetry. Seeing the stark steel surfaces brought back strong, familiar memories from years ago when I prepared my mom's make-up. Yes, the emotions returned as fresh as I thought they might. A white curtain was strung overhead, separating Kathy and Kadin like a hospital room. They each lay individually on roll carts, with their necks supported, with warm-looking covers draped atop them.

I would prepare Kathy first. Approaching my sister, I looked at her face and she looked at peace now, not at all showing the ordeal she had endured that ended her life. The trauma marks I had seen in the ambulance were now gone from her face.

My friend said very little and stayed at the foot end of the cart, still very much by my side, leaning on the steel cabinetry. I glanced at him sympathetically as he held his hand over his mouth perhaps in concerned astonishment that I was doing what I was doing. I appreciated everyone's concern that I should not be alone while choosing to prepare them, but I understood, too, how it might be hard for him to support me and watch as I go through this. I forewarned him that I would be talking to them just like they were here with us.

Kathy's dark hair was very soft to my touch, and I ran my fingers through it. Her long naturally curly hair fell framing her face. I chose to pull some of her damp newly washed ringlets back from her forehead, to show her beautiful features, and fasten the gathered hair with one of her own barrettes. For her jewelry, I put earrings that had horses jumping through horseshoes into her pierced ears and put a natural stone beaded necklace on her neck. We had made necklaces together at a church function once, and I gave her the one I made because it suited her best. It brought joy to me when she wore it because it was special between us. Now, she would wear it forever.

Kathy loved her horses, so I knew she would like to be buried in her hunter jumper show attire, and the family agreed. Her light blue-buttoned blouse, fitted navy jacket, and even her tall shiny black riding boots were perfect.

Kathy looked so sharp and regal when she rode horses and jumped in competitions that I wanted her to look splendid even in death. To add to the horse ensemble, I made sure she had on her fun "horsing around" socks inside her boots. Looking at the socks on her feet made me shake my head, sigh, and give a strained smile. Her feet were always, so cold so for my own peace of mind the thick socks would be most comfortable. "These will keep your feet warm, Kathy."

My mother had preferred brighter make-up shades where my sister mostly preferred natural colors. I stroked on a palette of brown eye shadow, neutral lip color with a hint of pink, and an ever-so-light pink tinged to her checks. She really did not need much make-up, even now- as her face looked utterly angelic.

Going around the white separation curtain, I saw my nephew for the first time since the tragedy. With a heavy heart, I looked at him. "What happened?" I thought as a tear filled the corner of my eyes. I knew in this life that the question would go unanswered.

Kadin did not need much make-up to his face because he already had a deep base coat applied. There were, however, a few touches that I thought to make. I would give him rosy cheeks- just like they always were in life. I took some hair mousse and worked it through his hair watching it shine. Kadin was high energy and was always gleaming from sweat because he played so rough and tough.

I said my goodbyes to them and knew their bodies were prepared for burial with the cosmetics now complete. They could be placed together side by side at last.

CHAPTER 10

Heavenly Slumber

We do not want you to be ignorant about those who fall asleep, or to grieve like the rest of men, who have no hope. - 1 Thessalonians 4:13

We opted to have the wake at Hope Church as Kathy and Kadin had grown to love the church so much. Without a doubt, it seemed to be the perfect place. The decision to move the viewing from the traditional funeral home parlor was a wise one, as our family did not realize there would be countless mourners paying respects.

Indeed, the funeral service would be difficult for our families and the community. Nonetheless, on autopilot we continued with the sorrowful preparations for the funeral service.

* * *

Recently, I had begun placing some of my abstract paintings at church to enhance the walls in the gathering area. My gift of painting has brought both blessings and personal joy when I use it to make religious artwork. My contemporary painting style seemed, for a church setting, forbidden and foreign because I grew up with elaborate angels floating on heavenly clouds, ornate and detailed. I always felt a special reverence for the sanctuary area in our church and did not feel worthy to paint a picture for the virgin walls.

Honestly, I could not conceive my abstract, expressionistic work to be church worthy. I believed it would be impossible that anyone viewing my work would be able to garner anything significant from looking at the paintings. I have since learned that notion is misguided. People comment about my paintings often, and I did not realize the impact they would have on the body of Christ at church. My thinking was narrow-minded, I supposed.

I had just completed a large painting of Jesus as he was baptized in the Jordan River. The painting showed Jesus emerging from the river with water running down his body. I had been talking with Kathy about the painting, getting her input, and was planning to show it to her before it was hung at church. As always, I needed her final say that I was headed in the right creative direction to reassure me.

Kathy never saw this painting completed.

I wished the painting to be hung for their funeral service. Friends came together and hung the painting for me by the baptismal tank just left of the stage and the casket. What would Kathy have thought of it? I painfully longed for the answer.

The immediate family had gathered many photos of Kathy and Kadin, mounted them on foam board, and placed them on pedestals throughout the building. Framed pictures and poems were displayed for people to spend time reflecting on the memorable moments of their lives. Baby pictures, vacations, birthday celebrations, everyday life, and loved ones who had passed all affixed. I was the safe keeper of oodles of our childhood photos after mom had passed. Going through the photos was heart wrenching because there were so many years' worth of memory-filled stacks of pictures of Kathy, Kadin, and my mother.

The horse painting my sister had created on canvas and some wooden cutouts of heavy construction equipment Kathy had painted as wall decorations in Kadin's room were prominently displayed. My dad had made Kathy a custom wooden bench to rest her saddle on, so we placed the bench up front along with her English saddle, crop, and riding helmet. For mementos of my nephew, we placed his football, his baseball glove, some yellow construction toys, and his royal blue church vest complete with the patches he had earned for learning Bible verses.

* * *

The casket arrived by hearse and was placed near the front stage alter as planned. With the casket open and readied for viewing my sister and nephew lie - side by side. We placed my sister's flannel horse print pillowcase, taken from her bed, over the traditional silky pillow in the casket. Sweetly, Kathy and Kadin looked like they were just lying together peacefully taking a nap, just resting on the horse pillow. "How I wished that were true," my heart sank. Kadin had his green Army man and Pokémon card tucked partially into his pocket. In the fold of his arm rested his blue tattered teddy. We tussled his shirt a bit just as if he had been at play. Kathy had her arm wrapped around Kadin and the other hand held her pocket Bible and a set of her drumsticks.

Kathy's love of the drums had started early in her childhood. One special Christmas, when I had just turned 8 years old, my favorite gifts were a life-size Baby Crissy doll (which grew red hair out the top of her head) and an Operation game. My sister, who was all of 5 years old, loved to watch re-runs of The *Monkees* television show on Saturdays mornings, and loved to imitate the drummer, Mickey Dolenz.

So that year, Kathy got a special gift at Christmas- a new Mickey Mouse and Donald Duck starter drum set complete with a real metal symbol. She would beat on her drums and together we would act out a Monkees episode while we played the Monkees LP record. We had so much fun together singing the theme song "Hey, Hey we're the Monkees and people say we monkey around…" I suppose the Monkees' music had an influence on Kathy as a child. Since she took great pleasure in drumming practice on her starter drums as a child, that could very well be why she so enjoyed playing the drums as an adult. Her love of playing the drums continued all her life.

When we first started to attend church, I remember sitting in worship one Sunday and whispering to Kathy that I had an idea how she could use her gift. While we focused on the music team during worship, I whispered how awesome it would be for her to play drums during the service up on stage. Kathy whispered back, "Karen, you are nuts because there is no way I'm good enough or could get up in front of people… there aren't many girl drummers." I knew I would just love to see my little sister up on stage beating on a drum for Jesus. What's more, I knew my sister had a temperate touch and could stay on beat so she would play great. I just had to encourage her to try. Though she was apprehensive in the beginning, she stepped out of her comfort zone and became an integral part of the worship team. The worship team became a special place for her to serve using her gift.

* * *

Behind the casket, up on stage, was the drum set assembled as Kathy would have played them during Sunday service. Wooden drumsticks were fastened together to create a cross and then attached to the snare drum. The drumstick cross was backlit to show a larger shadow of a cross-projected onto the wall. It was a touching gesture from the worship team's other drummer. Kathy had told me on numerous occasions how she so admired his drumming skills.

The funeral preparations at church continued with flowers arrangements and live plants arriving to fill the sanctuary with fragrance. Since it was winter in the Midwest, seeing such colorful foliage was unexpectedly uplifting. The church family was incredibly hospitable during our family's time of great need with every aspect of the service dotingly attended to. They truly loved on us.

Kathy had made a very special friend who was a vocalist and also on the praise team with her. They often joked with each other, and designed artwork for church when needed. He and his wife specially designed the programs and printed them with Kathy and Kadin's pictures on it for the funeral services. The program was a touching tribute to Kathy and Kadin.

We selected a verse at the funeral home during the planning for the "In Remembrance" card. The sentimental verses suited the two of them so well.

We'd like the memory of us to be a happy one. We'd like to leave an afterglow of smiles when life is done. We'd like to leave an echo whispering softly down the ways, of happy times and laughing times and bright and sunny days. We'd like the tears of those who grieve; to dry before the sun. We'd like the memory of us to be a happy one.

Happy…

It is hard to think of those happy times and laughter while fresh with grief. Nevertheless, the words were very fitting for both Kathy and Kadin.

The day of the wake, thousands of people came to pay their respects. The community grasped what a huge loss our family suffered. It was overwhelming. There were few dry eyes as mourners passed slowly by the sole casket and saw Kathy and Kadin side by side.

Close friends placed notes, sports jerseys and keepsakes, teachers and classmates shared stories, and teammates of Kadin's approached the casket as a team in uniforms. My older nephew Keegan's, teammates gave him a baseball jersey signed with sympathies for the loss of his little brother.

Our family stood for hours accepting condolences. Granted, we were all so tired and in shock it is difficult to recall all who passed by us expressing sympathy. It was easy to see that some mourners were extremely uncomfortable and at a loss for words as they made their way by the casket. I saw distress in their facial expressions, a sincere outpouring of tears mixed with horror over their drowning deaths. We heard many caring expressions to try to console our broken hearts. However, all the words run together when one is functioning on very little sleep.

"Please accept my sympathy."

"I'm sorry for your loss."

"You're in my thoughts and prayers."

These sympathy lines should give the griever comfort, and they do to a point. Yet, when I heard these words hundreds of times I began, to look past the worn phrases. I looked intently into the peoples' eyes, making some noticeably uncomfortable I gathered. Even so, I gained something greater appreciated from them than the cliché verbiage they said. Instead, I sensed, "I really don't know what to say… so sorry you are hurting."

After all, this candid line of sympathy really makes more sense to someone experiencing heart-wrenching loss. There is very little the person can say to make the griever's immediate pain cease. The loved one will not return. The fresh wound endures.

Another common phrase is "They're in a better place now." This expression tries to slip past the woefulness one is experiencing and give the griever hope. For some, a better place indeed is promised after death. This place of Paradise would be without sorrow, sadness, or tears. Nevertheless, for plenty of grievers, this "better place" would be having our loved ones standing right beside us, very much alive.

I sincerely said "thank you for coming" and accepted countless hugs. Honest and genuinely kind words were spoken to me during the wake. My mind though was foggy, functioning in a protective mode. Somewhat like observing an incident from afar, not really believing you are actually part of the tragic event. Indeed a "How could this be happening to us" way of thinking.

But, there was also a phrase that resonated and played again and again in my mind while standing during the viewing. "Why do you grieve as though you have no hope?" Those words from 1 Thessalonians filled my thoughts when my mind found a moment to drift. I fitfully looked into the crowd of mourners filling the church seats and then into the casket. This specific Bible passage kept me from breaking apart. It kept me from admitting to myself "I'm losing my mind because this is too much to handle." It kept giving me hope that there would eventually be some peace. Still, my mind projected back and forth from a sense of reality quickly back to the comfort of denial.

As the evening and line for viewing ended, our families were in dire need of some rest. Not realizing it , I had gone days since their deaths without sleep. I, however, had every intention of mourning into the wee hours.

I could not imagine leaving the casket. I felt such a strong desire to remain with their bodies at church. It was a lingering feeling, much like the moments of not wanting to leave the lake were they died. "I want to stay by their side tonight," I requested. There was little objection from anyone in regards to me keeping nighttime watch by Kathy and Kadin. In the company of my husband, we spent the night in our church home.

Indeed, there is something comforting about spending the night in your home of worship. How much I wanted to feel their presence here, God's presence.

How peaceful it was to allow my thoughts to wind down and have a bit of respite while sitting back in a cushioned church chair with my aching feet propped. I reflected on the wake. "So many sad people, I cannot believe all that came," I said to my husband. He agreed.

The sanctuary looked like a thriving greenhouse with hundreds of live plants, cut flowers, and roses. I had time now to pause at their sweet scents and appreciate their beauty. I went on a self- guided garden tour, stopped at each arrangement, and studied its flowering composition. I awarded no prizes as they were each memorable and unique in theme and display. I held several of the tender blossoms in my hands. Sadly, I knew the cut flowers would only bud for a short while. The flowers reminded me of my sister, here on Earth for a short while to bloom with her beauty.

As I became more emotionally brave, I moved upstage closer to the drum set she loved to play. A funny little notion crossed my mind. "Maybe I can play loud enough to wake the dead." Sorrowfully, that would not happen. Picking up the sticks, I attempted to pound out familiar tunes we enjoyed worshiping together to at church and sang to myself - all while trying to keep somewhat of a drumbeat. I paid a musical tribute to Kathy and Kadin by playing the drums clumsily up on stage in the dim lit sanctuary. Kept tears stored up from the wake were welling in my eyes. I gave a little grin because I knew Kathy would be laughing at my drum skills by this point.

I wandered around the church halls aimlessly walking laps, mostly in darkness, whistling and singing, leading my own funeral processional. The hall corridors echoed and I forgot I was in fact singing alone. The church had graciously prepared a family room, from one of the student classrooms, for us to take breaks in during the wake. The family room came complete with a full spread of finger food and drink, which was donated for the family. We were able to take very few food breaks, though.

I couldn't recollect the last time I had sat down to eat a meal. Wandering the halls, I felt like I was a child again waking up with hunger pangs needing to sneak into the fridge to- raid it late at night for a snack. Food leftovers from the wake were kept in the church kitchen, which I also found my way into. I opened the stainless steel door to the refrigerator to see the feast of foods before me. I had to admit I was feeling weak from not eating and had a dull headache. Unfortunately, my mind was sending me a mixed message, a confused message. Something inside me made me feel guilty for eating. "Did my body want me to starve and deny it food?"

I was at the point where I needed to close my weary eyes and at least try to rest. What I did not anticipate was I was headed for a spiritual meltdown. My husband had already been sleeping across padded chairs in the first row but I ambled into the church sanctuary prayer room to see if I could find rest. I had spent many a Monday night having small group prayer time here. My puffy eyes were very heavy indeed, but my mind would not allow the sleep to begin. Then I decided to grab a pen and write God a long note…

Taking the ink to notebook paper, I pleaded to know why this unthinkable tragedy had happened.

"WHY GOD… WHY?"

I wrote down all my deepest thoughts and love for them, which was forever lost. "You knew my sister was all that was left of my mom." I pressed violently into the paper, page after page and wrote all the ugly thoughts and agonizing emotions that spewed out of me, just pleading for answers and to understand why our families had to endure such suffering and sorrow.

I could not believe that, even though I was empty, I found sentences to fill with praising God, giving Him glory, asking Him to use this situation in a mighty way.

It is a hard thing to grasp, when loved ones die without warning and you find yourself wanting to be used by God. Used for what? "What do you want out of me?" I shouted into the room. "How, God, could you let this happen?" I remember hearing people make that very same comment at the wake. I considered that for a moment and grew confused at how I was not so incredibly mad at God like I would have the right to be selfish and angry.

"It's not His fault, the world is fallen," I slowly spoke softly in dismay answering my own question.

Dark ink continued to flow from the pen mixing with moist tears dropping to the page making it difficult to read what was written. Even so, the emotion in the writing was clearly visible. The time was now somewhere past 4 o'clock in the morning. Experiencing complete mental anguish, I returned to Kathy and Kadin's side after pleading and inking my points to the Maker.

Jeff restlessly slept stretched out on the cushioned chairs. He too had very little rest since their deaths. I tried not to disturb him as I peered quietly at them both in the open coffin. I leaned in and touched Kathy's hand and rested mine on top of hers for a few moments and blew kisses in the air. I felt an outpouring of emotions for my sister and nephew and spoke, "I will miss you all the days of my life."

My shaking legs were telling me standing was becoming less of an option so I lay down next to the casket. Here I prayed and sobbed in stillness on the carpeted floor, listening only to the church sounds at night. The inner sanctuary had very little outside light, which could only be seen from clear panes of glass from the entry doors. This night, the only additional light source came from two floral arrangements up on stage. These electric branches, wrapped with tiny yellow blossoms, were left on to softly illuminate the sanctuary. As I rested, I gazed intently into their glow.

As a child, I remember how Kathy and I needed the security of a night light -we were frightened of the dark. When we became afraid at night, we would both run as fast as we could out of bed and to the safety of our parent's room. Our dad was a state trooper so he would do shift work including working through the night. We would get scared sometimes without our brave dad there to protect us. On those occasions, Kathy and I would take the square pillows off the couch and line them up all around mom's bed to makeshift comfortable sleeping spots on the floor were we felt safe - camping out.

When we were sometimes banished to our rooms, the closet light most definitely stayed on with the smooth pine sliding doors open a few inches allowing a stream of light to enter into the dark. Sometimes Kathy or I would sneak past mom and dad's room and crawl into each other's bed making tents with the blankets for security. I had a canopy bed so I would take strands of

Christmas tree lights and string them around the frame for added illumination.

For sure, the little Kohler girls were afraid of the dark. When we got a bit older, we each adopted a more mature source for light at night. I would turn on my red lava lamp, watch the red wax flow and shape while Kathy turned on the multi-colored disco lights from her electrophonic stereo.

* * *

I knew Kathy and Kadin were now in an intense, brighter, and protective light and unafraid. But for me, little night-lights from the floral display in the church would have to suffice for light, and yes, I was very much afraid of life without them. While the tiny bulbs faintly glowed, I briefly drifted to sleep at Kathy and Kadin's side.

CHAPTER 11

Celebrating Death

*You learn more at a funeral than at a feast—
After all, that's where we'll end up. We might
discover something from it.*

Ecclesiastes 7:1-3(Message)

As emotionally difficult as the wake was, the funeral and burial would be equally hard. Everyone's prayers were lifting us up so far and I knew those prayers had held us up together as a family. I prayed this somber funeral day would still be seen as a celebration of Kathy and Kadin's lives.

The church was filled to capacity for the service with very few chairs, if any, to spare. As is the traditional sequence of funeral events, I knew the time was drawing near for our family to say our final goodbyes. One by one we filed by Kathy and Kadin. I leaned over and whispered, "I miss you both so much. Save a place for me, OK?"

Physically seeing my loved ones in their bodily forms for the last time on Earth was personally the hardest part of all. I would never look upon their beautiful faces again. The casket was closed for the last time… I closed my eyes.

Oh, how I remember so vividly seeing my mother for the last time before her casket was closed. She was wearing a champagne-colored chiffon dress, which next to her dark summer skin made her look like a radiant angel. We fastened a strand of pearls my dad had given her years before around her neck. Mom was humble when it came to things like expensive jewelry. I know at times she sacrificed her material wants so Kathy and I had plenty. Modestly, mom always seemed content with less for herself.

Nevertheless, we decided to buy mom a pair of new earrings for the funeral. We shopped and chose a pair of pearl jewels, clip-on type that would complement her ensemble. Mom also resisted any notion of having her ears pierced even though it was becoming very common. She did not really wear earrings unless she was going somewhere very special with dad.

Mom was not enthusiastic about having my ears punctured either. It was not until high school that I was allowed to get my ears single pierced after much begging. Since I survived having my ears pierced, Kathy was allowed to have hers pierced, at a younger age, when she was still in junior high. Still, when all the girls were getting their ears pierced back in elementary school, I decided to creatively improvise since I wasn't allowed to have mine pierced. I would cleverly take tiny round seed pearls; the kind inexpensive necklaces are strung with, Elmer's glue, and paste them to my earlobes. It was messy and time consuming, but to fit in during those awkward years I had to be resourceful.

* * *

I knew Kathy and Kadin's funeral would be a mix of people and religions. During the planning for the music, this religious meld was taken into consideration. The worship team Kathy so enjoyed serving on performed familiar hymnals. Traditional songs, *How Great Thou Art* and *Amazing Grace* were played with electric guitars and drums with a contemporary beat. My husband, who also plays on the praise team, paid tribute to both of them by playing his acoustic guitar for the first few songs of the service .I knew it would be difficult for him, and it was.

I sat composed in my chair in deep thought during the funeral. Friends and family went forward and read Bible readings with words of undying love, endless faith, and everlasting hope.

My mind was once again filled with the scripture and the question that had been constant for me since the beginning of the wake. "Why do you grieve as if you have no hope?" More than anything, I knew the words should bring reassurance. I could just hear Kathy saying to me, "Karen, be happy for us. Don't be sad. You know where we are. We were good and faithful servants. We have our reward, so don't grieve for us-celebrate!"

Death does have a different meaning when you are a Christian. But when it comes right down to it, I am still human and the pain of missing them was fresh. I found myself going through moments during the service where I was genuinely smiling while wet tears formed and fell. More than anything, I wanted an uplifting service were Kathy and Kadin's lives were celebrated. I was at peace having faith and the promise to trust where their souls were, for sure. Not just hoping if I pray for them, or have others pray, they might be found one day ready to get into Heaven. They had arrived.

The service continued with a testimony from friends and a eulogy by Kathy's brother- in-law. Both were touching and sentimental. I knew my humble sister and nephew would be smiling just hearing what was being kindly said. Pastor Darrell gave such an inspired message, and I listened intently as sincerity and encouragement poured out from him. While he was honoring God and remembering Kathy and Kadin, I prayed silently for him to have strength. What a burden had been placed upon him during these past few days. He was called to be the shepherd who was to give hope to a church full of mourners while he himself was mourning with us.

I had felt led to ask my pastor during the planning for the funeral service if he would offer an invitation for anyone who wanted to accept Christ. Kathy would want as many people as possible, especially immediate family, to have a personal relationship with God the way she and Kadin had.

Up to this point, I resisted turning my head to see the people, the sad faces, behind me during the service. If I turned and saw everyone looking at us through tears, I knew I would not be able to hold myself together and would completely break down. "God, help me," I whispered. I would save falling apart for another time when I was alone. I did not turn around.

Then the worship team played two contemporary songs *I Will Rise* and *Praise You in the Storm*, which was the song I softly sang while kneeling by Kathy's bedside the night they died.

As the memorial service was nearing the end, I had managed to outwardly suppress my emotions (the best I could) for the past few day to get through the funeral preparation. These had been the saddest days of my life, but I just had to see to it that Kathy and Kadin had a funeral fit to commemorate them. In reality, deep within me, I wanted to scream aloud and wholly break down in tears every moment along this ugly journey. But I did not.

The pallbearers, wearing white carnations, gathered around the casket to escort them to the waiting hearse outside of church. There would be a police escort, a pleasant surprise, to the gravesite led by our childhood neighbor who chose as his career to become an Illinois State Police officer. I turned to go down the aisle to follow the processional, but now I could not avoid facing the people sobbing. I sang along as the hymn played all the while keeping my eyes fixed upward. I could not bear to see the horrible harshness of grief.

* * *

Kathy and Kadin were buried in the cemetery where my mother, grandmothers, grandfathers, and so many other departed relatives lay in peace. Following the burial, everyone from the service was invited to a meal back at the church. Many of my relatives experienced firsthand the love the church had for Kathy, Kadin, and our families as we all mourned their loss. Family and friends shared stories of Kathy and Kadin while we ate together. Hearing stories of those precious moments made me smile, and my heavyhearted mood began to soften.

Before the sun would fully set on the funeral day, we wanted to return to their grave. I looked at it as if we were going to tuck them in for the night. Following along the cemetery's gravel road, we turned a few corners, passed rows of headstones, and spotted the fresh site. Their grave was covered with newly turned soil, and cut-flower arrangements from the wake were placed atop. The earthy smells of dirt and flora filled my nostrils as I took several deep breaths continuing to hold in my grim emotions as we stood graveside.

"Maybe this is a good time and place for me to have a long cry?" I considered, as if the option to cry was all in my control. Pitifully, I was trying to plan not only when I would cry, but also where I would cry. Was I really trying to control when I cried? How miserable I am, I reflected.

The sun had disappeared at the skyline and the moon had begun to ascend behind me, casting a beautiful soft light into the night. While standing at the new grave, I could clearly see my mother's stone marker when I looked forward a few rows of stones. Noticeably, the moonlight beamed brilliantly off the front of her stone so I could locate mom easily by reading K-O-H-L-E-R. The bright light reflected strikingly only off her stone no others in the row. How perfect and comforting that marvelous light was and I held to myself, "it rather divine." I shook my head slowly in wonder with a half grin on my face, I imagined the awesome celebration as all the departed friends and relatives greeted Kathy and Kadin upon their arrival.

PART

II

Death's Aftermath

CHAPTER 12

What Happens Now?

Every hardship; every joy; every temptation is a challenge of the spirit; that the human soul may prove itself. The great chain of necessity where with we are bound has divine significance; and nothing happens which has not some service in working out the sublime destiny of the human soul. - Henry Fielding

Unanswerable questions ran through my mind over the following weeks. "Does life just pick up where one has left it before a sudden death?" I wondered. "What am I supposed to feel like?" "How will people react to me now?" These and other questions scrolled in my bemused mind - post funeral.

My house, lamentably, looked much like a funeral parlor. Cut flowers, which were starting to fade, would shortly wither and die, just like my sister and nephew, I grimly reflected. The growing plants would need care to stay green and live. But I didn't have enough energy to care for them and keep them alive. How would I even help them to flourish while I was personally wilting, no, I had died, inside.

What energy I could muster, efforts, and concerns centered on other family members, and how they were coping weeks following our heartbreak. For now my husband and my tween-son mostly fended for themselves. My nephew, my brother-in-law, my dad, and stepmom were always in my thoughts. My married daughter was expecting her second child, another little boy, and I worried how the trauma of losing her aunt and godchild would affect her pregnancy.

I dreaded leaving my home...

I was not ready to resume life on the outside as if nothing major had happened. When I finally would rally the mental energy to even consider leaving the house to do a short errand, I would run into someone who would stop me in a public place. Indeed, I would be put in an uncomfortable position and asked personal family queries.

Questions such as "How are your dad and his wife doing?" or "What about your nephew and her husband?" "How is everyone holding up?"

"How are they doing?" I registered the general question. Really, what was I supposed to say? "Oh, they're all doing, just great!" It would be a lie to respond as such.

I became increasingly annoyed and irritable with people and their questioning. Frustration and then annoyance continued to escalate. I was having increased resentment.

As a protective measure, to guard myself against unnerving empathy, it became easier for me to say to others,

"Fine, they are all just doing ….fine."

Interrogation would usually cease as they realized I was avoiding a detailed response .Still, I always felt they were expecting to find out more intimate family particulars.

Well-meaning individuals would also say expressions such as, "My thoughts are with you and the family," or "I've been praying for you. I don't know how you're doing it- staying so strong." This is a confusing statement. I would think if they had been praying for me, then they knew how I was staying together. I was further befuddled. What kind of thoughts are you thinking if you say that your thoughts are with me? "How can you possible know what my thoughts are -doesn't make any sense."

"I can't imagine your loss," were words I heard frequently and retained. Truthfully, I could not imagine my loss either. What I did want was to imagine they did not die, that there was no loss. I could barely mentally and physically function living in such immense despair pretending our loss was not real temporarily deadened the pain. Sadly, there was no denying it.

I had people tell me "Kathy would not have come out of that water alive without those boys. How could she have lived with herself?"

This was such a heavy statement to make. I just could not comment.

Soon it became apparent to me, through people's comments and questions asking about my other family members, that I was just the sister who lost a sister and nephew. Few people gave the impression that my grief, being only the sibling, was as …extensive. I felt alone and forgotten as a griever.

I even felt forgotten by God. Why didn't I feel Him close and comforting? I closed my eyes at the end of each day and prayed to Him to let me feel He was with me and cared. Still nothing.

Why was I trying so hard to stay strong anyway? I felt so emotionally frozen.

Mostly, I lacked any useful grieving skill for discussing my unimaginable sorrow at this point so I mentally opted to stay in the comfort of denial for however long I needed.

I could not brave going to church services like I attended routinely, any longer. There were far too many memories of Kathy and Kadin.

Seeing the drums she enjoyed playing up on stage was painfully crippling. Besides, I did not want to talk and fellowship with anyone because I was buried in so much hurt. I needed to come to terms with my personal hell. I wanted to be left alone with my own thoughts but never got that opportunity, as well-meaning people ran to comfort me if I started to look sad. "Just leave me alone," I wanted to say, but I wasn't strong enough to respond in that manner.

So, I would act strong when I did make it to church, give off a signal that all is fine, and "Please don't disturb me I'm worshiping." Inside, however, I was withering. I wanted to just sneak in and out of service, but that was not possible either. I would use the side entrance to church (and I still do) and avoid the front entrance at all cost because people might talk to me. My inner introvert found a corner to settle in, pushing the normal extrovert from the scene. I was afraid to endure the church thing.

In my grief, I thought about how various cultures wore black garments to indicate they were in mourning. I would have welcomed that practice so that I would be left alone to fade away when I went to church or was out in public. Surely then others would see the attire and give me needed space.

The faith and hope I thought I held so strong was ...fading. I knew I was failing as a fresh griever. "Where was my Savior?" I had a horrible void in my heart, and I wanted God to fix and fill it immediately. What was He waiting for? "I very much needed him...

I became very confused in the wake of their deaths.

For self-comfort, I'd listen to my Christian radio station, Joy FM, even though I was hardly feeling joy these days. The inspirational tunes and talk stirred my emotions. My sister and I both listened to the same station so when I heard songs we particularly enjoyed, the pain of her absence gripped me tight.

I couldn't stomach deleting her cell number and name from my phone. I'd scroll through my contact list and see "KATHY," and I ached inside. I tried calling Kathy's cell phone number and act as if I was talking to her about everyday things, but the number was already disconnected. I pretended then. At home when I was alone, I began joking and talking aloud to her like she was just within earshot in another room. Hoping and waiting on her reply. Still, silence, no answer, no comfort. I would scream in agony for God - still silent, no answer, no comfort from Him either. They did not survive and I felt like I wouldn't survive either. "I'm dying here!" "Just dying…"

* * *

Since they passed away in February, the winter weather proved to be the gloomy backdrop I welcomed to complement my feelings of hopelessness as time carried on without them. Consequently, I chose not to leave the house for anything less than going to work. I was not compelled to go outside in the dead of winter much anyway.

I was exhausted and I was sleeping… a lot. It took so much energy to even get out of bed on some days. I thought if I were sleeping maybe I would get some revelation in a dream to provide comfort. But nothing miraculous occurred during my hibernating sessions to bring relief from the extreme sadness I was shackled with.

Other family members were having dreams of Kathy and Kadin when they slept, which brought them comfort, but personally brought little to me. If anything, hearing their happy dreams of Kathy and Kadin exasperated me. Again, I was forgotten even when it came to being given sweet dreams.

I've always felt that God speaks to me in dreams because I do not slow down enough for Him to get a word in during the day. Truly, I've had intense dreams that impact my daily life and that- I won't ever forget.

After my mom passed away, I had one of those powerful dreams, which give instant, unbelievable peace. This distinctive dream, or state of being, was truly an out-of-body experience. The significant dream gave me complete hope and encouragement that all was well with my mom's soul and I would eventually the heartache would subside.

In this dream, I looked down over my body and observed that I was asleep, under the covers in bed. Next, I was inside my body sitting up in bed. I then turned my head back to see that I was still sleeping soundly on my pillow. "Wow," I recall thinking in my dream state, "This is cool. I can see my body, but I'm sitting up, looking at myself sleep!" I turned my head, in ultra-slow motion around to the left to see my deceased mom sitting right next to me on the bedside.

She smiled at me, and I noticed she had her natural teeth not the replacement set she had once she had gone through radiation. In just her smile, I felt an extreme, warm love overcome and fill me. She looked younger and healthy, like I imagined she would have looked prior to her cancer, which ravished her earthy body. I remember thinking she was about my current age at the time, 23. She wrapped her right arm around my waist and telepathically said, "Oh, honey, I'm fine." She looked intently, directly into my eyes, and I felt her convey without words how distressing it was to see me sad.

When I awoke, I had a happy rush that I absolutely knew I had communicated with my mom. To this day, just recalling the intuitive look she gave from her brilliant blue eyes brings me hopes, filled with tears.

So why hadn't I been given a divinely inspired dream of Kathy and Kadin like I had with my mom to comfort me now as I navigated into the unknown?

A simple dream was all it would take for me to be reassured and keep going on with my ugly life after loss. Instead, dreams filled with voids of nothingness and despair plagued me. There were mercifully no nightmares. Because I felt continually troubled, I had a hard time getting quality long-spans of rest while I slept. I cried out nightly in desperation for the purpose of their deaths to be revealed to me... nothing. My nightly dreams continued to be filled with nothing but utter emptiness.

Somewhere deep in my inconsolable despair a small reassuring voice was whispering, "Brighter days are ahead… Karen." I sighed. Before their deaths when I wanted to feel close to God I would simply paint. "If I painted again would that soothe deaths sting for me?" "Would God then come close?" I considered that pacified outlook.

I picked up my paintbrushes and struggled to create again, but the emotions I was experiencing since their deaths proved to be more dismal when slapped on canvas. I was painting the repulsiveness of grief-and it was not pretty. God had given me inspiration to paint specific paintings in the past, why nothing clear to paint now, just muck. Perhaps I was not divinely destined to ever paint again, I mused.

Grief ridden my mind was stripped bare, but still I threw paint on the canvas even with the lack of inspiration. Blood red hues and black washes covered the canvas with images of screaming faces, chilling crosses, and thick drips of paint showing my raging state of mind. My last two paintings, painted the night of their deaths, seemed so divinely inspired. Now, my painful moods could not help but be dreadfully displayed upon canvas. "Please, God, I am afraid to paint my **repulsive** feelings." In anger I threw the paintbrush across the room.

CHAPTER 13

Birthdays and Butterflies

A butterfly lights beside us, like a sunbeam...
and for a brief moment its glory
and beauty belong to our world...
but then it flies on again, and although
we wish it could have stayed,
we are so thankful to have seen it at all.
-Author Unknown

Despair and depression continued unceasingly to strangle my entire being in the weeks that followed Kathy and Kadin's deaths. I was spiraling downward without care of reaching an emotional bottom. I began to believe that I was going insane. I certainly felt like it.

I found little joy in the things that once brought me happiness. "I don't even want to be happy," I told myself. I tried to tuck all the pain deep inside, so when I was around family and friends I gave the impression that I was back to normal, or at least what they felt my normal was. However, I was far from feeling status quo.

My dearest friends remained a constant source of support. I was sealing off from others, but those closest to me experienced the day-to-day heartbreak and pain along with me. It was all consuming now. They never let go and they stayed by my side, whole-heartedly listening to me when I did muster the energy to spout.

Kathy's birthday was March 26th, just a little over a month since the drowning's. On the first birthday without my sister, I sat and reflected what the day would have held for us had she still been alive. I would have taken her to lunch, and she would have ordered some type of veggie something or a healthy whole grain flatbread wrap. She would have iced coffee or unsweetened tea. Once the tea arrived at our table, she would pull from her small purse her personal stash of natural Stevia sweetener packets.

She would then tell me all about the horse item she was going to buy with the birthday cash I gave her or we would take off and go shopping so she could select her gift. Still, I always gave her a little something as a keepsake, be it a card or a sentimental gift, to let her know I loved her.

Kathy and I often talked about our age and growing old together. Without having mom and grandparents alive, we had little idea of what the aging process could have in store for us physically. I told Kathy jokingly how lucky she was because she could see what ailments might come next because she could see what happens to me. I knew my health-conscious sis would turn the tables on the aging process by the healthy measures she took on a daily basis.

One thing I could tempt my sister's healthy taste buds with was one of my hand-decorated cakes. She very much enjoyed splurging and eating the high- calorie butter icing.

I made Kathy a special birthday cake for her 40th –the last one I would ever bake for her. As traditional over-the-hill cakes go, the cake had black bordered icing with green grass covering the top. There was one special candle, which I had recycled from my 40th that now rested on my younger sister's cake. The special candle, a wax tombstone, read, "Here lies my youth…40" This cake, which was supposed to be all in fun, now deeply disturbs me as she would never see her next birthday.

I did not anticipate my sister's 41st birthday to be a pleasant day for me. Even though I wanted the day to quickly pass, a good friend surprised me with an adventure. I was not ready for an escapade especially if it were intended to bring me enjoyment. This would be the first year without the birthday girl and the day would not be one I wanted at all to enjoy. Nevertheless, she whisked me out the door after work that day, into her car, and on the road, we went. I was very reluctant to go because at that point the thought of doing anything for fun just did not resonate well with me.

We had the most perfect adventure in my sister's honor - birthdays and butterflies.

While driving to our outing, I learned the surprise destination was an observatory for butterfly watching in St. Louis, Missouri. Even though in March butterflies are not flying in the air where we live, they were indeed flying abundantly in the controlled climate of The Butterfly House. The greenhouse was abundant with butterflies, but they were not just random assortments of butterflies.

Butterflies remind me of my lovely sister-the way they float so gracefully beautiful. Kathy was indeed graceful when she was effortlessly poised atop her horses or while creating a beautiful work of art. The wind carries a butterfly in so many directions, up, downward, and then up again all while maintaining balance. My sister managed to kept balance with her family, household, church, and on her horses.

Not just any butterflies remind me of Kathy but especially the Blue Morpho butterfly. This type lives in rainforests and has strikingly brilliant blue wings. To my delight, the month of March at the butterfly house featured the Blue Morpho butterfly. "How coincidental," I said surprisingly. The house was brimming with the flutter of blue wings.

We stepped into the tropical environment, which included lush emerald and lime-colored leaves, trickling water features, and tropical flowers in full bloom. Pebble paths led to hidden areas with tucked-away bench seating for resting and reflecting on the tranquil beauty all found inside this warm, glassed oasis. The air inside smelled earthy and moist with faint scents wafting from the blooms.

Seeing thousands upon thousands of blue butterflies, all in fluttery flight, was emotionally overwhelming. The butterflies would land on my arm, slowly close their wings, and open them as if they were waving hello. Seeing the butterflies, experiencing the kindness from my friend, warmed my heart.

What a respite for a grieving soul. Green plant life abounding in the humidity with the striking blue butterflies resting on the foliage was peacefully picturesque.

* * *

A Morpho butterfly was the choice for my sister's permanent body art. Kathy had a small tattoo on the outside of her wrist of a blue butterfly in flight. I always thought the tattoo was impulsive but still beautiful.

I have seen some intricate, well-designed memorial tattoos and decided as a tribute to my sister I, too, would get a tattoo on my wrist. Kathy would not believe that I would even have considered a tattoo. She told me she got hers to disguise a scar on her wrist. As part of my grieving, I decided to have a chic blue butterfly tattooed on my wrist, too. I told my father I was going to ink a butterfly and he said without hesitation, "I will, too." My dad getting a tattoo was the most spontaneous and unpredictable thing I had ever known my dad to do. Certainly, my dad had experienced a life-altering change, too.

I helped design my dad's tattoo with a banner draping across the butterfly's open wings with their names and date of death crossways on the scroll. He had the butterfly inked on his shoulder in patriotic red, white, and blue. Our tattoos are memorials of Kathy and Kadin that we will always share. When I see the blue butterfly on my wrist, I think of them. The tattoo is my eternal ink.

Soon, spring would arrive giving way to warmer days, and bright green growth would start to peek through the landscape. The red bud trees and daffodils were starting to show color and the bleakness of barren sticks was being replaced with blossoms. Warmer weather meant that I no longer would need to panic when I saw a frozen lake or pond. In fact, the pond they all perished in did not re-freeze that year. I was hoping with the change of seasons that I could shelve my sorrows. Sort of, tuck grief away my deep feelings until I was ready to fully deal and accept the magnitude of my loss. I ultimately found out grief simply does not work that way.

Sharing all of nature's beauty with my outdoorsy sister was something I would never have again. Kathy and Kadin enjoyed the country life on acres of land that offered spacious grounds to engage in family recreation. Four wheelers, motorcycles, large pastures for the horses to gallop, a creek to explore, lots of firewood for bonfires, and ponds for fishing, all could be outdoor amusement. Their property was like a vacation campground hidden in the woods.

As kids, my sister and I often asked to sleep in our tent in the backyard. We had a bright orange tent that slept four people so we would pitch it and for fun have neighbors over for a sleepover. Board games, flashlight tag, scary stories, snacks, and secrets were all a part of our tent time.

As the weeks passed since their deaths, happy memories of our childhood would suddenly be in my thoughts

Celebrating our birthdays, eating hot breakfast cereals at the dinner table, riding bikes with playing cards fixed with a clothespin to the spokes, and even quarrelling as we cleaned our rooms, those memories make me melancholy now. Those once-meaningless memories of everyday childhood routines are deeply cherished more than ever. Life, priorities, all change after the death of a sibling.

* * *

If nothing ever changed, there'd be no butterflies. -Author Unknown

CHAPTER 14

Needs Neglected

Suffering produces endurance, and endurance produces character, and character produces hope. -Romans 5:3-4

Grief was taking a damaging physical toll on my health. Days were filled with fatigue, yet nights continued to offer inadequate and restless sleep. I struggled with lethargy, fluctuating mood swings, and general physical exhaustion. I functioned with a slight but persistent headache along with heart palpitations or racing heartbeat, which sent me into paranoid panic. "I feel like a part of me has died with her." "Oh, please, surely I must be dying." Oddly, I accepted the alarming physical discomforts as life post Kathy and Kadin. My health was being gradually depleted.

My need for food was constant, and I never felt satisfied after eating to eliminate my hunger. I felt emptiness in my stomach…and heart. Through self-diagnosis, I determined that I was dehydrated most of the time, causing my body to be unbalanced. I began making some very bad food choices- ones with empty calories. Food became an available source of quick yet unfulfilling comfort. I was unaware of the bodily sabotage as I packed on pounds - but couldn't have cared less. My metabolism was non-existent.

As kids, Kathy and I had our favorite treats. However, even with the high-calories we consumed, we always stayed slim. We drank RC Cola and sang the jingle, *"Me & My RC"* or drank the astronaut drink Tang or chocolate Ovaltine. We enjoyed eating Chocodiles, Pringles, and Marathon candy bars, as tasty energy when we took a break from playing. We ate tasty cherry Luden's cough drops by the box, not realizing it was a sore throat medicine. We could eat what we wanted without much consequence, except for frequent visits to the dentist.

We would hop on our bikes with our neighbors and ride for blocks just to walk up to the window and order ice cream at the small town creamery. Banana splits, hot fudge brownie sundaes, chocolate and vanilla twist cones all tasted delicious on a sunny day while sitting on the curb chatting with good friends.

Our cold breakfast cereal choices were often between our favorites Quisp and King Vitamin, to which we added real sugar by the spoonful. When the cereal was finished, we were pleased to have the sugar- laden milk to sip at the end. Together we sifted through full cereal boxes till we found the toy prize promised inside. We also liked opening the little package of instant oatmeal and adding hot tap water. But on Sundays, a big breakfast featured Mom's biscuits and homemade sausage gravy.

To this day, biscuits and gravy remains for me an ultimate comfort food.

I mourned them so and attained quick comfort in those familiar foods from our childhood. I even made Mom's recipe biscuits and gravy for my brother-in-law and nephew. I should have known that Kathy's healthy standard of eating would not have offered biscuits and gravy on any breakfast menu in her home regardless of what we liked as kids. She strived to ingrain healthy eating habits into her family, and she wanted me to adopt a health-conscious lifestyle, too. I had lots of work to do.

So, I was not surprised to learn my fit sister had never prepared the carbohydrate-loaded, sodium-sinful dish for them. I prepared it special for them and they enjoyed it nevertheless.

Since Kathy's passing, I was haunted by guilt when I ate something she would have found- unhealthy. It was as if I heard her voice saying, "Don't eat that, it's so bad for you." Yet, my new eating routine was skewed as I convinced myself that I might as well enjoy the food because I might die soon. The "I don't have much time to live" mantra was an easy excuse to justify my harmful food choices. A will to live life before their deaths was now being replaced with a desire to give up on this life, one unwholesome bite at a time.

* * *

Largely, I suppressed my inner-most feelings of sadness and would not let the grief surface long enough to bring it to a point of dealing and healing. I felt like I had lost touch with others. No one could understand my pain of loss anyway, so I chose to distance myself. The meaning for my life, for my purpose on earth, was very much unclear at this point and became heavily clouded by dark thinking.

I needed my sister…

We were connected in life as sisters- why not continue that connection in death? I wanted desperately to hear Kathy's voice, feel her presence. I became even more sad and dejected when that failed to occur. I fully believed that she would somehow contact me from beyond the grave. "Kathy, I'm waiting…"I would whisper. I just could not understand or come close to accepting her not "visiting" me. When I mentioned casually how I hoped she would appear to me, some responded by saying she could not because it was not of God. I know all things are possible- so I held on to that possibility.

But not receiving any concrete assurance of an after-life made me feel spiritually inadequate. "This is all there is…"I'd reflect. Overpowering torment continued to work on my mind to fill me further with spiritual doubt.

I saw myself as pitiful and repulsive. My dismal thinking pattern wanted to usher in potentially destructive ways to harm myself. "Why am I constantly having self-destructive thoughts?" I'd contemplate. I also believed I was rendered unworthy of any future happiness and therefore useless to society evermore. Remorse from sin many years ago that I had long since been forgiven and forgotten was resurfacing. Mistakes and regrets that I was willingly allowing to become fresh again… guilt building upon guilt.

Through all this self-hate and confusion, I still longed deeply for comfort. "Am I being unreasonable?" I missed my sister so much that physically I found some tangible comfort holding her possessions. My brother-in-law while he was working through his grief asked me to clear their closet of her clothes. I took her personal things to my house in plastic tubs, which I would sort through sometime in the future. Having her stacks of clothes around, which would never fit me, wearing her make-up and spraying her colognes brought on the memories and brought me temporary grief relief. I knew I would never be strong enough to put away all her belongings. It would be like forgetting how important she was to me. I wanted to keep them "alive."

I think I can relate to how compulsive hoarders may rationalize keeping what they do. I held sentimental value in Kathy's ordinary objects. I developed terrible anxiety of letting go of anything that was once my sister's and supposed that if I did, I might in some way forget her. The pleasant memories in my mind were not "touchable" but holding and touching something of hers brought me warm contentment. I gradually dispersed some of my sister's clothes to friends in the hope of seeing them wear them, which might bring back happy recollections.

The reality that they would never return to use their belongings caused me to experience further emotional numbness when I held onto denial. "Would I ever be able to fully step out of my painful veto of going through grief?" I was not at all sure. The pain was gripping me at my core – I was comatose and was beginning to believe I had waited too long.

As time went on, the burdening emotional turmoil within me gave way to more ongoing physical pain. "Why can't I ask for help?" I felt increasingly tired and overwhelmed by even the smallest home chores my energy was depleted. My thoughts became foggy, more forgetful, and I had difficulty remembering anything that was not an absolute essential. Even with shopping lists, I would forget basic items, though I usually forgot the shopping list at home anyway.

Grief brings with it many…. experiences. I could not work through my feelings. I began to be subject to panic attacks where I felt I could not stop my hopeless feelings and had totally lost emotional control. Fortunately, these attacks occurred in the privacy of my home when I was alone with my thoughts. My body would break out in a heated sweat, with a racy heartbeat, and I found it difficult catching my breath near - hyper-ventilating.

My breathing would then become shorter and even more irregular when I realized I was in this state of panic. I experienced a strong sense of doom. My eyes would travel rapidly side to side as I came to the reality I would likely never be mentally stable.

At times, I experienced paralyzing fright when I was by myself. "Do I want to be around others… but I really don't?" I juggled. But I was lonely. I would not allow myself even in seclusion to break down and cry my eyes out. I became agitated even more easily by little stressors, and was frustrated by my unshakable irritable mood. "Why am I losing control?" "Deep breaths," I would tell myself.

My close friends stayed by me and were much- needed support team willing to let me slowly vent my misery at my own pace. I believe they were the crucial part that kept me from breaking completely apart. I was in crisis. My family loved me, but I was very moody and could tell they were becoming increasingly frustrated with me. At the time, I didn't know I wasn't OK.

I tried desperately to sidestep grief, but I was failing. Grief was confusing and all consuming. "Is grieving just simply having a good cry?" "I just don't know." Even during my worst emotional mania, I held back tears. "I don't want to experience grief..."

CHAPTER 15

Emotional Meltdown

Never apologize for showing feeling. When you do so, you apologize for truth.
Benjamin Disraeli/ Prime minister

Fraught and desperate to feel less emotional and physical agony as the days past, I was having difficulty separating facts from fiction. My thought process was warped. What I did not realize is that I had become so depressed and disassociated that I was voicing aloud, (not just in my head anymore) that I wanted to end this life. I wanted so badly for the pain to leave me. No amount of pleading prayers had brought me the peaceful comfort I needed to regain a will to live life again without them.

If anything, I felt like a spiritual battle between good and evil was being fought, and my soul was the prize. I knew what side I had intentionally joined but was not sure why the coach had decided not to play me in the big grief game. Maybe I was being red shirted to give myself time to get back in the game? Or was the coach deciding to trade me to the other team? No, I was prolonging accepting grief and giving into it. I was stuck maintaining my bench warmer position.

I continued to have ominous urges that seemed to infiltrate my mind telling me to do harmful things to myself, to take the pain away forever. I found myself in darkness.

I could not understand in my heart why God did not seem to want me anymore. "Why doesn't He fight for me?" Had I gotten that off track? All I wanted was to be loved so deeply and told everything was going to be fine. I had that loving peace when my mother died, but why was God so distant to me now? I begged and cried out for Him. Was He listening?

My friends, family, and co-workers saw my mental deterioration. What I did not comprehend was how much they feared for me. In my fog, I did not see the things they noticed and heard me say. Without realizing it, I continued to mention how I wanted to end my agony. I wanted life to be over, a done deal.

A little voice of evil whispered constantly inside me. It was unyielding in pointing out my hopelessness. Without my sister, I felt as if I were only half of me. Many of my childhood and adult memories would never be talked about again because there would not be any fond reminiscing like, "Do you remember the time", or "remember when we..." between sisters ever again. Any memories I had were for my mind only. There would be no one to share those sister times with.

What of a future could I now have without my sister? She listened intently to my continuing life dramas and only commented to interject what God's Word would demonstrate truth. The truth for me now was borderline insanity with the mental and physical breaking point nearing.

* * *

A very strange and unexplainable thing happened during these dismal days.

I was at home in my kitchen ready to eat something and decided an egg and cheese sandwich sounded fine. I went to the refrigerator, took a new package of cheese slices out, and set the package on the countertop. The cheese package was unopened so the outer cellophane crinkled as I tore my way to the contents. I discarded the outer packaging and went for an individually wrapped slice.

What I found between my factory-wrapped cheese slice was unexpected.

Between the slices was a corroded box cutter blade.

"Huh, is this what I think it is?" I picked up the used blade, trying to put a reason to why a dull razor blade was in my sealed cheese package.

I stood in the kitchen bewildered and tried to solve the mysterious puzzle. Perhaps at the plant, during packaging, the blade somehow made its way into the wrapping area. Consequently, I just so happened to purchase that exact cheese package. "Wow, what a fluke," I briefly deliberated.

I was baffled. Holding the razor blade, I walked into the next room still very confused. I approached my husband and asked, "Did you put this rusty old blade between the cheese slices so I would find it and kill myself?" His response was,

"Woman, you're crazy!"

I silently contemplated his response as I headed unhurriedly back to the kitchen. Was I? Was I really crazy? "Maybe I should just really end it all," I thought.

Then to my surprise I recall hearing a deep, menacing voice in my mind goading me. I heard this ugly voice loud and clear.

"Go ahead. Here's your chance to stop the pain!"

Oh, how I wanted to stop the pain… In my mixed-up mind, I envisioned myself slitting my wrist with the sharp rusty blade, drop my arm to my side and saw the bright blood trickle down from my wrist and drip from my fingers. The thought was oddly acceptable to me and not as terrifying as it should have been.

I did think about doing it…

I left the house to go to work as usual. Throughout the workday I mentioned my sliced cheese discovery to my co-workers friends who gave me distressed looks. Unbeknownst to me, an alarm had been sounded on my behalf. Those close to me wanted to get me some mental help. I soon grasped that my box cutter comment was of concern to all of them.

CHAPTER 16

Pain, please don't find me

There are some things you learn best in calm, and some in storm. -*Willa Cather/Author*

I was scared to seek any professional help. I maintained I was "above" ever needing that "sort of thing." I was paranoid and in distress of what others would say or think about me. I thought I should just abandon the notion of getting pain relief and getting well again. "Was I really sick?"

Had I reached my bottom? I felt utterly empty.

I was disconnected, and my outlook was nothing but bleak. My body had physically rebelled. I was losing hair by the handfuls and easily gaining weight. I was exhausted and incessantly sighed. My joints painfully ached, grey hairs sprouted where I had few before. My body had dramatically aged.

Through loving, concerned, and convincing tears from those closest to me, I halfheartedly agreed to seek counseling. I told those plotting against me I would do it eventually, hoping by saying "yes" they would leave me be. I didn't know what measures my friends had in mind to find me professional assistance to rid me of my death wish. "I'm fine," I told everyone. But saying "I'm fine" was no longer convincing for my inner circle.

It took candid persuasion from a close friend through sincere tears to finally sway me to get the help I needed. After I finally agreed, he ardently played chauffeur. I looked at the car ride over to the suggested center as a new adventure. What an adventure it would soon become.

The hospital appeared to be at first glance a peaceful place, nicely decorated like a hotel lobby at a Holiday Inn. I spoke to the smiling receptionist at the concierge desk who directed me to another seating area. This one was definitely not upscale. This lackluster and uncomfortable looking room promptly put me in a defensive mode. In my mind, I was formulating a clever scheme. My plan was to appease everyone who was concerned and just talk to the professional for a little while. I wasn't the least bit concerned as I knew I would be soon leaving because nothing was mentally wrong with me - so I believed.

I couldn't help but notice that the waiting room's décor had dated walls, mauve chairs with permanent coffee stains on the fabric, piles of last year's re-read magazines, and an outmoded television that hung in the corner inaudibly broadcasting. I was becoming more apprehensive about agreeing to be here, especially when I noticed a security guard frequently made rounds up and down the hall. "OK," I inwardly plotted, "I will just smooth talk my way through this and show the lynch mob there was nothing to be concerned with."

I was summoned into a private consultation room where I was evaluated by a counselor. I told her how much I missed my sister and nephew, that they died by drowning along with my nephew's friend. Then I told her about finding a razor blade unexpectedly between my cheese slices. To my surprise, she suggested after talking with me that I check in for a while. I was reluctant because I was much too busy to "check in." Begrudgingly, to please those closest to me, I agreed to stay, just for a bit. I anticipated my stay would be much like a vacation. Maybe this was all I needed- time off for grieving? I did not yet know what I had gotten myself into.

"Was I about to take a big healing step in my grief?" I considered. What I really wanted was to not take any steps at all and just run far away. Oh, how I wanted to step away from this sorrow and just escape from my horrible reality. Here, I now found myself forced to take steps to process my loss, my grief - in a hospital.

Going through the conventional textbook steps like denial, anger, bargaining, depression, and acceptance do not always apply as straightforwardly for unexpected loss. No, losing someone to sudden death is more like playing hopscotch. Grievers jump over steps, then return to another step, and go jumping back and forth. These established steps are often referred to as a grief journey or process. For me as a griever of abrupt deaths, my grief journey wasn't a customary one.

When family members die suddenly, how can the torturous numbness of losing them in anyway make sense? Death makes no sense to the suffering soul left to live. You were not ready to let them go anywhere and there was no warning they were not going to be around tomorrow. Instantaneously, one is thrown into a surprisingly intense hurt.

* * *

My family and friends left me at the hospital to get better. "Can one get better by grieving?" I proceeded with the standard admittance process.

After a full pat down to see if I brought along anything illegal or harmful to do damage to myself, I was given a pair of light blue scrubs, top and bottom(very familiar attire for me), leaving my street clothes with the warden to be locked away. Any personal belongings such as a comb or make-up were also kept. This admittance process was far more intense than I had foreseen. I was just waiting for the security guard I saw pacing the floor earlier to escort me to my cellblock.

I was placed in a stabilization unit for the deeply depressed and suicidal. The space was definitely not the restful retreat I was almost looking forward to visiting but was actually harsh and was indeed more prison-like.

My room was modest. There were no decorations or lamps and just a curtain to the bathroom. No television to keep me entertained, just solitude. "Oh my," I commented. Looking about the unpretentious room brought on a flashback of my high school religious retreat, which was held at a monastery for the priesthood. The large door to my room was not allowed to be completely closed, and had to remain slightly open at all times – just open wide enough for a nurse to enter.

Yes, the room was deliberately safe…

The single bed, I was assigned to felt lumpy and tested noisy as I sat upon it. . Tossing or turning from side to side at night would surely wake one from the squeaking springs. There was a large window in the room, but there was no curtain to give any privacy. "I guess privacy can be dangerous." I snickered. I would not have the unadorned space to myself because I had a roommate. Her bed was closest to the door. I wondered if her mattress was as objectionable as mine because she rarely left the comfort of the covers. It took some effort to reach out to her and be friendly, but I tried.

She really did not get out of bed much. I felt empathy toward her because her days were spent sleeping and weeping in the hospital room. When I asked her how long she had been in this place she said, "What day is it?" I told her it was a Friday. She looked very puzzled and slowly said, "I don't know how long I've been here." Here replies were causing me to experience some extreme anxiety. I cringed, "Would her lacking state of consciousness soon become my own?"

Checking into this place was intended to protect me from hurting my bodily self. It would be far more difficult to protect me from hurting my -mental self. I realized that even with all the protective measures to ensure my safety, it would not be so easy to shift my pessimistic thinking process. Thus, my observant mind was focused on becoming acclimated to this hospital and to quickly learning the ropes.

Hunger pangs gnawed at my stomach and I soon discerned food was about the only choice I would be able to make for myself here. "When is lunch?" I questioned. Inopportunely, food was served only at certain times, which meant it would be difficult for me to binge eat. "Great, no more eating a dozen cookies in the closet," I thought ruefully.

A nurse entered the room to fill me in on the timetable of things during my stay. Everything seemed to run on a schedule, which was good for me, as I like to know what to expect. This nurse's sole duty was to take my blood pressure and temperature. After she recorded my vitals and removed the tight cuff she over inflated from my arm, I asked her in repartee fashion "am I still alive?" She obviously had no sense of humor and did not comment or even look my way as she quickly entered notes in my chart. "Nice," I asserted. "Now, I already have a strike against me." The nurse instructed me to go eat some lunch as she made a half-waving hand gesture.

It appeared the patients, seated around the table, liked to watch the attendant, dressed in all white scrubs, wheel in the stainless steel food trays at the designated time. The attendant muttered under his breath as the stainless coverings rattled as he wheeled. The high-pitched pinging sounds from the trays clashing together sounded much like brassy symbols at a concert. At the time, I did not know this event would become a highlight of my stay here as well.

The dinnerware consisted of divided plastic trays and paper products. The eating utensils were also plastic, no metal knife or fork here. What food you chose to eat, or not eat off the plastic plate, was tallied by an attendant who watched us the entire time we dined and scribbled notes in charts. I was sure they were writing, "Patient did not eat her peas, however the chocolate pudding cup was completely consumed."

During the designated meal times, I met some of the "regulars." Clearly, this was not their first time in this facility. They actually seemed to enjoy it here. They would ask, "What are you in for?" I listened to the "sentences" of others before I figured out why I was incarcerated. Many were recovering drug and alcohol addicts. Some were manic depressive, severe paranoia, or schizophrenics. I figured I must fit into one or more categories. I just had not been diagnosed yet.

After lunch, I met with my assigned psychiatrist who really did not say much. He just wrote a lot. He did not ask me challenging questions, but he always looked at me puzzled like he was working on trying to figure me out. I told him about my life in a nutshell. "My sister and nephew died. I feel like I want to die, too." Now that I had the required psychiatric session under my belt, I was ready for medication. "Maybe all I needed was some good drugs anyway," I truly considered.

Medication dispensing was another time to meet up with my new friends. We all waited in a single file line while a nurse dispensed cup after little clear cup of medications from her silver serving tray. I wore a fashionable hospital bracelet, which the nurses scanned frequently, that tracked my medication on a screen, showing what was dispensed. I figured they had all our information on that band just in case we forgot who we were while we were in here. I could honestly see that happening.

While the nurse watched me, I swallowed down my meds like a good, obedient patient.

After my first round of meds, I decided to return to my luxury suite to rest up for the next fun-filled day. Upon entering, I saw my roommate curled up in a ball on her bed crying. Seeing her disheartened face, I felt so sorry for her. I plopped down on my bed hard just to hear the squeaking springs for my own amusement. She did not even notice.

Even though the room was simple and uninviting, I noticed that there was reading material - a Bible. "Well," I pondered, "what better place to have the truth told." I picked up the book before bed but the old wording of the King James Version was challenging to understand as my medications began to truly kick in. I opened to the book of Job, I think because I felt we had pain in common. I read a few chapters then my mind started to …drift.

With my new pills, I had a flood of grandioso ideas and reasoned my medicated mind could solve much of the world's plights. I felt a free - almost floating - sensation and my vision became blurry. I lay my head down on the flat but lumpy pillow because I began to notice I was feeling light headed. My body felt very warm all over. I thought it best to shut my eyes for the night.

* * *

Sunrise brought sunbeams glaring through a window without curtains. "So much for sleeping in", I snickered. My roommate was already up and staring out the window. Not trying to invade her space, I asked her casually, "What do you see out the window?" She did not turn or move in any way, but she responded, "My family is coming for me today." I answered back, "That's great!" She managed to smile at me.

"What was on the agenda today," I wondered, as I rolled over to my side on the wretched bumpy bed. Just then, an Asian nurse came bounding in to record my vitals. The first words out of her mouth as she reeled about my room caught me off guard.

"Karen, you're not going to kill yourself today, are you, Karen?" "NOOOO, you're not going to kill yourself today, Karen."

I think she was waiting for me to answer, but I had to chuckle inside a bit before I responded. Then I answered her with, "No, I don't think so."

My nurse shook her head up and down, wrote a note on my paper chart, and then informed me that counselors led classes daily for the patients to attend. Great, I proclaimed, something to do!

When the time for the classes arrived, I realized they were not actually mandatory. Still, I wanted to investigate and hoped I would learn something earth shattering or at least get a star for good behavior for attendance. The interactive classes were on different topics with group discussions and handouts. I immediately noted the bizarre comments from the in-patients who actually attended the sessions. Some of the responses were so off topic, I wondered what drugs they were taking. I hoped that my new prescription would not cause me to behave so oddly.

Once again, a line formed with me tossing down -more meds, different ones this time, in different amounts. I swallowed them as told. I noticed I was again getting awfully dizzy but did not want to miss mealtime. Meals were an interesting diversion from thinking about my pain and sorrow. Besides, food was comforting. Since there was not much else to do here, I did think a lot about my pain…hunger pain.

As the dinnertime show began, I heard a rumor that one of the regulars who believed he was a real-life Superman would be performing tonight. In reality, he was a military veteran. During our mealtime he scaled the tallest tower, which for us was standing on a chair. I quickly was cast into his production. He would talk to me as if I were a news reporter, his latest Lois Lane. I played along for fun, although I am sure amusing him was not in his best interest.

Some of the other in-patients, I discovered, would try to skip meals and had to be escorted from their rooms to the table. I later learned it was mandatory for us to leave our rooms. It was required every day. In our absence, the staff would search our space for anything they needed to confiscate. I envisioned a big chocolate cake brought in by somebody's mommy with a chisel, for a patient trying to make a break for it, or at least smuggle in a nice fingernail file for a little manicure.

I thought about how great a massage would feel, especially after sleeping on the lumpy bed. Because I keep a busy schedule, I typically do not take much time to pamper myself. But in the hospital trying to occupy time, a massage was an excellent wish. "Where was the suggestion box when I needed one?" I scoffed.

With a full-body massage not a possibility, I searched for other entertainment. There were coloring pages and books, which held my inner-child's artistic attention. With broken colors, I colored butterflies, flowers, and rainbows. However, when I asked the nurses at the station if I could have a pencil and paper, they grew suspicious.

"I just want to take paper and pencil back to the room and journal and draw." After nurse deliberation, my request was granted and I got a pencil and backside of a paper for charting patient notes. I was not going to get to very creative as I was given a short, dull, yellow pencil that was most likely once used for a round of 18 holes of golf.

Back in the main gathering area, fun would be picking up for the evening, so I wanted to take a short, two-hour nap so I would not miss anything. After going to classes much of the day, I opted to take a nap as so many others routinely did about this time. The latest round of drugs was making me very tired and very sleepy. Yes, I was fitting in nicely here.

I awoke and headed to the lounge to see what merriment I might have missed during my snooze. A puzzle, which had been put together numerous times, was once again resurrected from its torn box, and several people took part in the reconstruction project. I joined in. The problem was we were so medicated, all the pieces looked about the same and piecing them together became very frustrating. “I’m not good at puzzles anyway,” I shrugged, “lack of patience I guess.” It became even more maddening when the puzzle was almost complete and pieces were missing. I decided some deviant in-patient was bored and hid the puzzle pieces in their room so when the room police located the missing piece, the perpetrator would be thrown into... the special room.

I peeked into the "special retention room." The space was padded all the way up the ceiling and around the bed. What I wanted to do was just step into the room and punch at the padded walls. Since I am a martial artist with a black belt in Okinawa Shoriyn-Rue Karate, I thought this the perfect place to practice kata. When I asked the hospital staff if I could train in the padded room, they said it might be a bad idea.

They wrote in my chart ...again.

Bored, I returned to my room, went to the large window, and saw the sky was changing. The weather was turning ugly outside. The nurses did a room check and informed us there was a possibility for bad storms and possible tornadoes.

This evening would prove to be a rather busy one for the hospital. Soon, steady bells and shrill whistles sounded in the hospital as a tornado was sighted nearby. The hospital was now on weather alert and the patients were on lockdown. The nurses herded us out of our rooms and assigned spots to sit on the scratchy carpeted floor down the brightly-lit corridor. With our pillows and blankets, we lined our storm bunker. With all the drugs I was taking, I was sure the tornado would pick me up and take me to the land of OZ.

The threat of a tornado touchdown had the patients' anxiety levels peaking. Some cried hysterically, some babbled on about pricey storm damage, some just slept lying up against the wall. With the sound from the loud crashes of violent thunder, the military veterans took cover and avowed they had returned to active duty. I was just a spectator and took all the commotion in stride. Fortunately, the storm passed and spared the hospital. We could not return to our rooms however until the hospital security guard came to our floor and gave the all-clear signal.

Finally, we were allowed into our quarters again. The persistent lightning invaded the room and the rain smacked the window loudly. The raindrops lit with brilliant illumination cast a runny outline as I watched them trickle down the glass. The medications were at work once again making sleep easy even in the midst of the fierce storm.

* * *

My eyes slowly opened to see my roommate's morning ritual of standing at the window peering out. I lay in bed recalling her comments from the first day I arrived. She could not recall the day of the week or even when her family would be there to take her home. I sat up in bed and realized I had no idea what day it was or when I would be leaving either. "Would I see the outside again?" I became panicky inside and jumped out of bed only to find myself once again lined up for the daily morning dose of medications.

The mood-stabilizing medications took away the desire to end my life but even in this altered state, I knew this would be a temporary fix. I still longed to hide from grief and would forever miss my sister and nephew until the day I died. I came to the realization if I could not end life, then I would have to live it - eventually.

During the nurse's rounds, I asked how long I had been a patient. She actually hesitated to tell me looking at me as if I had asked her how much she weighed or something. "I believe it's been about three days," she said shaking her head leisurely as if she was trying hard to remember herself. I quickly followed with another question. "When will I be able to leave?"

"Oh, you just rest; you have been through so much," she said as she left the room,

"Wait," I railed at the nurse. "I have been here a few days and have no idea how much more I have to go." I argued the weekend was plenty of time for my tour of duty here. I voluntarily checked myself in. I later discovered they could have kept me anyway. The nurse returned to my room so I bravely asked her another question. "Can I go outside today?" She shook her head back and forth as if to say "not going to happen on my watch." I fell back hard on my bed pouty and displeased.

I was mulling over the prospect that I had virtually been pulled out of life. I could just stay so foggy minded on medications and waste away here that I eventually would be like a zombie. In my depressed state, I fueled the notion that I was not needed in society anymore. In fact, I discovered, hiding from life could be done, and I had actually accomplished it. I had essentially left my life.

My close friends and family visited me even when I was at the lowest point of my life. When it was broadcast I had visitors, I visualized greeting them holding a phone separated by a wall like the inmates in a detention facility. Fortunately, that wasn't true, and I actually spent time alone in a room able to speak face to face with them.

Walking down the hallway to see visitors was somewhat of a challenge. Walking felt more like a drunken stagger. Since I was taking mood stabilizers, stabilizing my footsteps was the difficult part. I was embarrassed, as I was not allowed street clothes until the psychologist said it was safe and appropriate. Showers here did not involve a razor, unless supervised, and the towels were a little over hand sized, at best.

I was so thankful to have family and friends who came to see me in the hospital, but I wanted so badly to leave with them.

"GET ME OUT OF HERE!" was my drugged plea.

I looked around the room for a camera or hidden microphone in a paranoid fashion waiting for a strait jacket to be thrown on me because of my negative statement. My sympathetic visitors all told me to "get better," "we love you," and even brought me incredibly tender notes to keep my spirits up.

My plea to them was still, "HELLO, can't you see I'm going CRAZY….no, crazier!"

I was woefully miserable when they left without me so I went back to weep in my room. I sobbed because I knew they loved me deeply, but

I could not just get better. What I suffered from was not an illegal drug or over use of alcohol issue like others here at the center. In my heart is where I hurt. I could not get better from my sister and nephew's death. No magic pill would help me through this grief process *-unless I was ready*.

I was feeling ill side effects from the medication late the next evening. I worked myself into an agonizing anxiety attack because of my agitation and was lightheaded. Freaking, I wandered down the hallway in search of a nurse to ask if the dizziness and irregular heart racing I was having was to be expected. I soon determined the nursing floor at night is low staffed, as the highly medicated patients are mostly sleeping soundly and do not require much nursing care.

As I ambled in a panic down the hall, a new patient was being admitted, which required all the night nurses to assist. I settled in the hallway, leaning against the wall to steady myself and watched the chaotic scene. A young man in a strait jacket had several police flanking him as he was escorted to the padded retention room. His list of foul earsplitting profanities along with slurred words landed him in the brink. "To think I could have slept through this excitement!" I softly giggled.

A nurse spotted me enjoying the festivities and returned with me to my room where she gave me water and reassurance. I fell asleep.

In the morning at breakfast, to my utter surprise, the disfavored fellow, with help, arose from the padded room. He looked as though he had slept like a baby in his mother's arms and seemed to be fully rested. I sat in amazement watching his debut performance as he ate breakfast with us as if he had not eaten in days. He shoveled in the victuals, and savored every bite while actually grunting. Sometimes he missed his mouth, trying to eat so hastily, that the food dropped sloppily all over his newly provided scrub wear. It became easier for me to see, no smell, which patients had been here for several days or even weeks for that matter. Greasy unkempt hair, lack of showers, and the same set of scrubs on for several days with old food droppings. Who really knew how long we were here?

At almost a week, I was going senseless from the repetitive boredom. For good behavior, and successfully acting unaffected by tragically losing my only sister and a nephew at the same time, I was being allowed to leave. The psychiatrist's stipulation before I could be discharged from inpatient care was I had to agree to attend two weeks of daily outpatient care and counseling sessions through the hospital. Anything, I begged and said "YES," on the spot.

CHAPTER 17

Identity Crisis

A sibling may be the keeper of one's identity, the only person with the keys to one's unfettered, more fundamental self.

Marian Sandmaier, Writer

I was happy to be going home, but my roommate was not so pleased for me. She was extremely enraged when she saw me putting on my street clothes and stomped right up the nurses' station demanding to be released. I saw an angry side of her I had not seen during my entire stay, and my heart broke as I saw a spark ignite in her that had not been there, I imagined, in some time. In a frenzied outcry, she raised her voice. "Hey, what about me!" she directed at the nurses who congregated to keep her calm. I hugged her goodbye and told her I would be praying for her and to keep her spirits up.

I walked out the front door and looked up to my hospital room from the outside. I saw my distraught roommate standing by the window staring out as was her usual habit. As we pulled away from the parking lot, I waved and imagined the number of roommates she had seen come and go and how disheartening that must be for her to always remain inside.

For various patients, I suppose hospitalization works. While in the hospital, the medically supervised care allows for safely discovering what combination of medication doses work to stabilize one as to not harm themselves or others. For me, though, when I "went free" out of hospital detention, I knew that I would act as "normal" as a person could and vowed no more hospital stays. I had come to know I never wanted to return to what could have been an almost permanent vacation for my mind.

I knew my way of life now would never be the same as what life was like before losing my sister and nephew. I was not ready yet to accept that things would never be the same, and I was scared to find out how different they would stay. Finding out meant my grief would need to lessen, need to start melting. I would gradually need to find out what life would demand of me as I tried living without Kathy and Kadin. All of the happiest and saddest memories of my early life were moments shared with my sibling, and I was afraid to make new memories without her.

My two-week penance from the hospital psychiatrist, to go to group therapy, began right away. I checked in and out daily at the center and attended groups, which unfortunately were not solely geared to grievers. Mercifully, I had an assigned counselor who was sympathetic. She met with me in private and remarked, "You're grieving. This isn't the place for you. You stick out like a sore thumb." She was right. She offered me useful resources, internet sites, and share groups that I could explore, which were intended for those who had lost loved ones.

Still, during the group sessions those two weeks, I did learn about behaviors, addictions, and a multitude of mental disorders. I met some manic, obsessive, interesting, hurting individuals, and understood how my grieving very much affects those around me.

While in out-patient therapy, I was required to continue to meet with the psychiatrist who had seen and diagnosed me as an in-patient. I came to understand that his words of professional advice didn't suit my situation much, which gave me little hope of finding my new normal.

During one session, I recall leaving his office thinking I could not believe he was licensed- or at least I came to believe grief was not a condition he was skilled at treating. "Maybe he grew cold from all the hospital patients," I considered because he was so blunt. I asked him sincere questions on how to deal with grief issues yet he offered me guidance, which was not comfortable for me to use at this stage of my new normal. I asked him how I could respond when outside people asked me about their deaths or how I was doing. He told me to tell them,

"Oh, I'm over that, because that is in my past."

Those words wounded me deeply. When he said the line, all I heard at first was the "that" part-twice. I knew I was certainly having a problem, but the "that" he was referring so nonchalantly to, was Kathy and Kadin's deaths, and I knew I was definitely not "over that."

This doctor, I felt, could not have cared less what my past was with my sister and nephew. I never went back to him for any therapy.

I felt resentment brewing when I gave more thought to his words and avowed he had no right to tell me how to grieve, even if he was a professional. No one had the right to tell me how to grieve or how to feel. My despair was now filled with a new feeling - anger. I was indeed stuck in my grief, and now resentment was added. I wanted to stay stuck here for now.

* * *

Separating my identity from my sister's would be difficult for me. We were always known as "Karen and Kathy" or "the Kohler girls" growing up. But, the "we, she, and us," was to be no more because of tragedy. To some degree, we were contrary, but that is what kept us balanced. Kathy was my little sister, and I was the big sister. I embraced my role as a protector for my little sis.

We were not opposite when it came to our faith. We saw things, like our spiritual beings, the same as we grew older, which made our bond that much stronger.

I visited or phoned my sister almost daily, which kept each of us in check. I found we were more alike when we were alone together. Dreams and convictions shared with another, so much like me as anybody could ever genetically be, with the same belief systems. There was so much good about my sister that I always admired.

Kathy was a motivator to call me to action, and a supporter once I got into a project. Now that she was gone, who would be my motivator? Sisters have a way (and a duty, I believe) to be brutally honest with one another. Comments that come from a sibling are not always kind.

Nevertheless, we take the criticism out of love and appreciate the advice as if our own brain was saying, "You're absolutely right. I should have realized that!" "What was I even thinking?"

Since her death, I felt some of the best parts of me had also died. What is my identity? What kind of person was I to become now? I felt pressure from others who commented I needed to "pick up where she left off." To assume that responsibility was dauntingly impossible for me to comprehend. People would say, "She died so young. Now you have to live her life for her." That caused me mental instability even thinking how difficult it would be for me to try to mimic and "be" my sister and still try to be "me" all at the same time. An impossible undertaking.

My loved ones missed Kadin and Kathy, and if I could represent a part of her still here on earth, then I would try. I knew I would never be I decided to I let my hair grow so it would be longer and naturally curly-like Kathy's. I dyed my hair closer to the color of hers and wore less make-up. I was very different, though, from my gorgeous sister who natural beauty always overcame.

I often imagined what my sister would do or how she would react in a situation and try to react as she might. I wanted to laugh like her. I soon learned I could never live up to being my sister, and that was even more disappointing. This kind of thought process was exhausting.

Hope was on the horizon as my pastor suggested a Christian counselor who he thought I would better mesh with. My pastor had met him at a Christmas party and said he had a sense of humor. That made me smile. I could not imagine sharing my past and present hurts, harmful habits, and hang-ups with just anybody at this point, but I considered a new counselor, especially someone who might make me laugh, worth the risk.

What was my identity anymore without my sister? That was the big question that now haunted me. It would take courage on my part and much time to answer that question

I recognized that my family and friends had to be growing tired of hearing of my unrelenting misery, so what a wonderful thing to have a licensed listener to dump on. In spite of past therapy disappointments, I set up a session.

I spewed out to my newest counselor my mom, Kathy, and Kadin's untimely tragic deaths along with the past garbage of my life. I still carried around plenty of unresolved issues that helped to compound my grief, so it required session upon session to tell my life story to him. Remarkably, he listened. I felt he really cared about me getting healthy and working through issues, and I felt safe in my weekly sessions as I downloaded my life.

We talked a great deal about grieving, and I asked if I was abnormal. I learned grief is multifaceted, and normal for one mourner may be very different for another. My counselor gave me assurance that I was going to be OK, which is what I needed to hear, even though I truly believed I would never be OK again. I looked forward to my therapy sessions because it was as if my counselor was shedding light on the unexplored side of my brain that I had yet to figure out. He challenged my thinking processes and even assigned me homework.

Some of my homework responses I did as paintings. He supposed painting would be beneficial. Painting was unexpectedly therapeutic, even though it was painful and I was highly unsure of myself. "Can I even paint again?" Just picking up a paintbrush, holding it between my fingers, brought on strong memories. I channeled my suffering, tormented emotions onto the canvas through the brushstrokes. In one painting, I put all the words I was feeling spelled out on the painting, and swirled paints with blue hues and darkness over the canvas. Words like: torture, agony, loneliness, frozen, confusion, and heartache. All my emotions muddied in a muck of paint.

* * *

Who was I without my loved ones? This was the question I considered necessary to discover the answers to in therapy. I was going through an identity crisis, much as if I had amnesia and had to start my life over. I forgot who I once was and was struggling to see who I would become without them in my future. What I knew for sure was that I was minus a nephew and sister and was a fraught soul trying to reform my identity.

When I was in my counseling sessions, I did not have to pretend to be as strong, but I still found it difficult to outwardly express emotions or tears. Kathy and Kadin's deaths, along with my mother's years earlier, had been major tragic changes in my life. These suppressed feelings were overwhelming and were layered over lots of profound pain. I took a little off the top each time during my meetings with my counselor, processing my heartache.

To go through life in a healthy and positive mental direction, I had a lot of work ahead of me. It is hard to look at grief as work, as a recovery process. At times, there seemed no end to the mental and physical misery and it was difficult to believe things in this life could possibly improve. What I did strongly desire was comfort and peace.

I am not one to actively reach out for help. Nevertheless, by finding a Christian counselor who was a fit for me, I placed myself in a position to begin to receive help and open the pathway toward receiving comfort. I remember at the start of therapy that my counselor said he would walk along side me during my grieving process. I had doubts because inwardly I avowed, "I hope this guy likes working at snail's pace 'cause he is going to have to be here for the long haul." I was not about to rush this grief thing.

Mature Christians would tell me God was right by my side through all these trials. The fact was I did not want Him by my side. No, I wanted him in front of me, leading me. Generally, I have a difficult time making decisions. Having God stand by my side would give me comfort. However, I could not imagine I would take any steps forward in my grieving without an uncomfortable push. My counselor gave me that needed nudge.

CHAPTER 18

Keeping a Connection

The best remedy for those who are afraid, lonely, or unhappy is to go outside, somewhere where they can be quiet, alone with the heavens, nature and God. Because only then does one feel that all is as it should be. *- Anne Frank*

Several months had passed and summertime was in full swing. I decided staying busy outside with my hands in the dirt or tending to flowers helped to suppress my sad spirit. I would also go outside with my dog and listen to the sounds of nature as we walked along. Birds chirped, geese squawked, and leaf blowers hummed.

How I wished nature could speak words to personally appease me. Then again, I had lost heart I would hear something profound from the heavens. It was just that I was sure by now I would have had a sign or a dream, which would have brought me release from my tormented bondage.

So, as time moved on, I saw what appeared to be grief relief for those around me. Had everyone so soon forgotten them? I wondered. Or perhaps they already had come across useful grieving techniques, unlike me, to miraculously deal with the loss. So, I continued in therapy to try to release my grief.

* * *

As the seasons changed, so did my grief. Autumn leaves, tinged with color, withered, and began dropping from the trees as a new season of grief was upon me.

With the cooler evenings, I knew winter would soon arrive, which greatly displeased me. I wanted to hibernate and just wanted to sleep so that the empty, numb feeling would come and go without me much noticing. But grief has not a season of rest.

I continued to take medications. Still, strong waves of emotion, which I continued to suppress as best I could, would slowly seep out on those close to me and during therapy with my counselor.

Not surprisingly, my family and friends asked, "So, how's counseling going?" Counseling was a slow process of healing, but at least I was managing to wake to a new day. If it is possible to weep on the inside not show on the outside, I did that continually. I just did not want to grieve. It hurt, and time, it seemed, was not the answer to healing any of my wounds.

I noticed the change from hot to cool weather, and noticed my firm faith from the past had grown from hot to lukewarm, as well. I wanted and had hoped by now to have been filled with comfort. I expected it.

The winter after their passing was especially harsh in the Midwest. There was more snowfall than the previous years, and the lakes and ponds were covered with ice intermittently all winter long. I live on a lake and just seeing the water and ice on the lake daily maddened my thoughts. The icy lake was a daily reminder of how my sister and nephew struggled for life - and that they had lost.

I would forever more hate murky bodies of water. Yet, I still could appreciate water when it comes as a gentle rain. When the rain trickles, the rain became the tears I could not shed. Water gives life, water takes away life.

* * *

After months of nothingness, of not finding an after- life connection with my sister or nephew, I wanted to see what other options might be available to bring ease to my emotions. So I searched for something second-sighted to console me and maybe give me answers.

I sought out a spiritual psychic who claimed to connect with departed loved ones. I was uncertain she would help me and remained skeptical after she offered me nothing solid as proof during her readings. Her findings were generic, and I was certainly disappointed. She didn't "pick up" on my departed family until after I brought them up. Then she voiced they were coming through her, to hug my heart, how profound. She channeled their spirits by holding my hands and told me they were going into my heart. Funny thing was I didn't believe I had much of a heart left or even if it could keep beating. I quickly recognized the costly psychic was not a personally good choice for me for finding spiritual grief relief.

Not giving up totally on a paranormal possibility, I purchased an electromagnetic ghost detector online like the ones I saw on T.V. I became a fan of watching all ghost hunting shows and was intrigued how the "other side" could contact with the living. If this EMF detector was a tool to finding spirits, I wanted to find my lost relatives.

I was just so mixed up in the grief mess that I felt it entirely possible that Kathy, Kadin, and whoever else wanted to make themselves known to bring me consolation, would be able to be recognizable. So I would turn the device on, stare at the glowing green light hoping it would turn red, and wait for the sound to alarm that an entity was present. The change from a green to red light on the detector meant that a "source" was near and some believe this energy is a spirit. "This might work?" I half-heartedly considered. I tried asking direct questions aloud with the detector set to "on" position ....no light....no sound.

I did not give up on the machine even though I did not have success. I talked out loud and to myself in hopes of bringing my departed family to visit. I would get very excited when I saw the detectors light go from green and turn red. "You're here!" I saw glimmers of hope and whispered, "Kathy, if that's you, thank you for being such a great sister." "Kadin, we all miss you."

I was indeed enjoying the "ghost hunting" that I had taken up as an ominous yet soothing hobby. I'm sure my sister would have been shaking her finger at me looking to the occult for comfort. The paranormal possibilities seemed to be giving me relief, in an altered way from the gridlock of grief.

When I couldn't connect with Kathy or Kadin by any metaphysical means that I had explored, I then turned to the natural environment.

I relished being outside and began to experience nature as if it were talking directly to me. I noticed anew all the smell of the outdoors, soil, the tree branches as they swayed, and the air making melodies with my wind chimes. The ting of the chimes tubes and the harmonious sounds was an enjoyable language I was beginning to decode. I could not see the wind blow the chime but I came to the understanding the wind is there even though it is unseen. With this thought I prayed my sister, nephew, mother, and all my departed loved ones were with me but just hidden from my earthly eyes.

I was letting myself feel and connect with my surroundings - it was pleasant. I would sit on my deck in the dark of night for hours looking at the sky filled with the twinkle of stars. I came to revere the full moon as magical. I would reach and strain as high as I could into the night air to reach for those stars. But I couldn't reach Heaven.

CHAPTER 19

What Sisters Conquer Together

A sister can be seen as someone who is both ourselves and very much not ourselves - a special kind of double. - *Toni Morrison Novelist*

When the weather turned cold, Kathy and I would seek the sun. We had gone on several tropical beach trips, just the two of us to get away together. Spending 24 hours a day for several days with your sister on a trip might be torture for some, but we just grew that much closer.

My career is very demanding, so I crave a trip planned around relaxation. On the flip side, my sister yearned for exhilarating excursions. She worked hard at her horse stable, but she still sought to get out and be ultra-adventurous. Going on trips with Kathy proved to always be something unforgettable that I wouldn't think to do on my own. She always wanted to do the thrill seeking sort of stuff, and as long as I had some beach time, I participated in the adventure. Though we each had different expectations of what a vacation meant, we somehow balanced the trip out satisfactorily.

Zip lining was one activity I hadn't the slightest idea why I had agreed to try. Four stories above Mexican treetops, over water, was not my idea of safe. Kathy said, "I think that sounds like a lot of fun! Come on, Karen, you will like it." We booked the excursion. Like was not the word I chose to describe zip lining.

The eco-tour took us deep into the Mexican jungle. We experienced eating tasty handmade tortillas and beans to eat- along with salsa. We snorkeled together in a rocky-edged cenote where the water was a bit chilly. Then it was time for the much anticipated zip line adventure.

We went to the landing area where I watched a man with sandals shed blood as he tore off his toenail when he tried to stop at the end of the line. Shoes were recommended.

Kathy and I put on our helmets and a battered safety harness, which never could have passed a safety code anywhere else but Mexico. The kicker came when they said, "Go grab a stick over there for your brake." "WHAT?" I said to Kathy. "Surely we aren't really using a stick as a brake." It turned out we really were to use the brake stick. Somehow, an ordinary stick seemed somewhat unreliable as a brake, and I definitely wanted to keep my toenails. The fun factor my sister had convinced me to try once was suddenly becoming more of a fear factor for me.

Nevertheless, I went with the small group to a wooden tower multiple stories high and started the ascent to the top. The first thing I noticed was that the wooden tower was wobbly. The second thing I noticed was the sky had turned dark and we were about to have an afternoon thunderstorm. I thought to myself, "Surely they aren't going to lead us up a four-story tower and then let us zip down a metal cable when there is intense lightning spotted?" I was wrong.

With each step I took up the stairs, I prayed a little harder. When we neared the top and the take-off point, Kathy was excited to go. I was petrified. I had Kathy go first so I could see how it was done. After she jumped without any reservation, she appeared to be having fun, and in the distance, I saw her land just fine, keeping all her toes. It was now my turn, but I also grasped that I was the only one left on the platform. I had second thoughts…

There was something very wrong about approaching an elevated edge and then just jumping off. This involves a lot of trust, especially in the equipment. In my case, a wood stick. I contemplated that perhaps zip lining may not be as dangerous in the United States as I found it to be in Mexico. My heart was racing, I began to panic. I turned to the man ready to push me off and asked him if I was going to… die. I wanted an answer to my question. He knew little English and shook his head back and forth almost as if he understood my hesitation. He did not respond and instead gave me mighty, forceful push.

I screamed at the top of my lungs the entire way down to the landing. I pretty much forgot what to do with the stick and more than anything I didn't want to be stuck in the middle of the zip line left to dangle four stories in the air during a severe thunderstorm. Amazingly, I made it to the end of the line in one piece, and kept all my toenails as a bonus. I survived zip lining with my sister and miraculously lived to talk about it.

Another sister-selected excursion was horseback riding. She was sure the outing would be lame for her, though, since the horses were trail horses. A trail horse, which followed other horses in line, was definitely a steed more my speed. However, what heightened my sister's interest was the promise of going right into the ocean while riding on the horses.

Now, I was already no fan of riding horses. I knew my sister's suggestion about horseback riding was for me to conquer an old fear. Once while I was at my sister's house, she put me atop her almost 17-hands high horse. I already liked riding horses on trails, but instead she was going to teach me her new style of riding -English. There is a big difference riding English as opposed to Western. After I hopped atop, I noticed a big problem. There was no handle horn on the saddle to hold on to.

The horse decided it did not like me on it and sensed my alarm. For whatever reason, the horse decided to gallop and take me on a little unrestrained ride around the arena. I had no idea how to stop the horse gone wild as Kathy was blaring some kind of instructions that involved my thighs. I decided to bail off the horse so down onto my back I went. My sister was so concerned with my fall and aggravated at me all at the same time for not listening to her directives. I survived but was shaken.

So, mustering up my courage I agreed once again to get back on a horse-all because of my reassuring sister. My horse appeared to recognize the trail just fine that meant I did not need to do much but hold the reins. Kathy thought ahead so we took apples from the resort buffet to feed the horses. I looked at this, extending the apple gesture, as a tasty bribery for the horse in hopes it would not go loco and buck me off.

My sister knew some Spanish from school, and she also knew horse lingo in Spanish. The rancheros let Kathy take her horse off trail and let it run. That pleased her.

We slowly trotted the horses to a hitch on the beach. Here the saddles were removed. Again, I looked at my sister and asked her how I was supposed to control and hold onto a horse without a saddle. "Aw," Kathy said, "Karen, you have to hold onto the horse's mane," which sounded simple at the time.

The horses remained in a straight line and entered the ocean. So far, so good, I thought. The surprise came when the horses were so deep in the ocean their muzzles were making noises and their heads were straight up sucking air. "Kathy," I screamed in panic, "Do horses know how to swim?" "Yes," she replied.

I held the horse's mane but was floating all over the place as the water got deeper. Kathy chuckled. "Wrap your legs around the horses back!"

"I already tried that!" I countered. Soon, I relaxed some when I realized if I fell off, I knew how to swim. The horse's nostrils spouted water as we floated along. I could tell all the horses really enjoyed the cool down from the sweltering heat. Once again, I survived.

Still another adventure was when she suggested a four-wheeler off- road trek. I should have become wise when we signed the lengthy paperwork about insurance, waivers, and damages.

On the deeply rutted trails, our group of eight in number drove their assigned four-wheeler in somewhat of an organized line - at first. What I did not know was the large four-wheeler, a Honda-Rancher 4x4, was exactly the model Kathy had at her stable back home. When we were younger our dad got us a red Honda ATV 90 three- wheeler, which I handled well.

With its balloon tires we plowed through the snow, jumped piles of dirt, and rode on only two wheels doing wheelies. This powerful four-wheeler however, which was much larger, might pose a bit more difficult to control than the motor trike from my youth.

"Karen, just follow close behind me," she said casually.

Kathy was an expert at driving her four-wheeler, and she left me in the dust - literally. A helmet was provided but no goggles, so all I had were my sunglasses to shield me from the flying, powdery dirt. I squinted with tears of laughter flying off my face, leaving a mud trail along my cheek as I tried to follow nothing but a thick cloud of dirt ahead. Kathy made her way to the front of the line so the dust screen was left by her fast-moving four-wheeler. Once again, when the Mexicans operating this excursion discovered Kathy owned the same ATV and was a capable driver, she was permitted to literally go -off road, much to her delight. She made her own happy trail and covered me heavy in dust, but I survived.

I was certainly the more cautious of the two of us. My sister had a way of talking me out of my comfort zone and challenging me. Kathy and I conquered many things together. As nervous as I was by the adrenaline adventures she suggested, somehow I always felt all would be fine when we did the danger together. Fear crippled me, but Kathy was my encouraging crutch to living life to the fullest.

* * *

CHAPTER 20

Grief Vacation

"Time is irrelevant-it is all about the moments"

-Karen Kohler Kaiser

When going through the grieving process, no matter what the circumstance of the death, it is common to hear from others that the first year after death is the hardest. During the first year, birthdays, holidays, and anniversaries come and go, each one bringing memories flooding back about those who have gone.

It is a common for goodhearted people to say "they wouldn't want you to still be unhappy." Nevertheless, when one is resistant to grieve you may find yourself, as I did, with the one-year anniversary of their deaths approaching and wondering, "I'm still sad" and "have I grieved yet?"

I considered that I needed to schedule a time to plan ahead and set aside time to grieve.

I helped others and saw my family healing, but I never felt myself moving along with life as others would have wanted or presumed me to be by this point. My understanding husband and family understood my need to get away to grieve, to escape, on the upcoming one-year anniversary of Kathy and Kadin's deaths. They were OK with me taking healthy time to get away.

I planned a tropical trip for an entire week with a dear friend who was willing to go on a - grief vacation. She however called it our escape from reality trip.

Passports in hand, off we flew to our destination - Puerto Vallarta, Mexico. I was not at all sure how mentally trying re-visiting Mexico would be, especially since my sister was with me the last time and we had made so many fond memories.

I was melancholy as we arrived in Mexico. I was reminiscing about how much fun I had with Kathy there. "I will have fun without guilt," I tried to tell myself. We had planned several excursions, and I was so looking forward to swimming with the dolphins, which was something I had always wanted to do. Our dolphin encounter would absolutely be a highlight.

My friend and I donned wet suits for the chilly water at the dolphin encounter. The trainer blew on his whistle to stir the dolphins and alert them it was class time while we acclimated ourselves to the water. The dolphins were so buoyant, quick, and smooth with a rubber feel to the touch. We commanded the dolphins with hand gestures, gave them fish treats, and then swam with them by holding onto the pectoral fins while the dolphin swam on its backside around the water. It was truly an amazing experience.

Another excursion we chose was an off-road adventure by way of riding in a large military jeep-type vehicle. The road was a dry, dusty, rocky- riverbed, and was extra bumpy. We flew dangerously out of our seats even though we were holding on to a harness strap. My sister would have enjoyed this jarring thrill ride. I stayed active during our Mexican getaway, but little reminders of Kathy and Kadin were not far from my thoughts -no matter where we ventured.

Our jungle jeep took us off the beaten path to a not-so-touristy destination- Sayulita Nayarit. This town screamed eclectic, and the creative artist inside me felt immediately inspired as we walked on the cobblestone streets. Vendors along the way looked like they had escaped to Sayulita and enjoyed a casual lifestyle not caring where their next paycheck came from. I was envious and thought what a dream to escape here, do my art and painting on a street curb next to a beach hearing the surf, not a care in the world.

Many of the merchants wares looked as though they threw clay or paint together, made paraphernalia, and called it "art." I appreciated the variety of styles, but, in my opinion, the workmanship needed much fine-tuning. We walked along the beachfront, which was filled with attention-grabbing beach goers. Frisbees flew through the air, beach umbrellas abounded, and thatched cabanas and restaurants added to the character of this place. Sayulita had a vibe I found enticing mixed with quirky.

The beach was not flat as the usual but instead sand piled in thick mounds, made walking difficult as we sank to our ankles with each step we took. Looking to the water, this was the place to learn to surf. It was filled with young surfer dudes who were having a great time catching waves and were willing to take a few bucks to teach you how to surf.

Then we noticed a village of tents. It was like a beach campground for nomads. There were groups of people sitting in circles on the sand playing guitar and singing. These folks were more like modern-day hippies.

* * *

The sunny weather was warm and pleasant, much different than the winter weather we were having back in Illinois. Our beach at our resort in Riviera Nayarit had glitters of gold flakes floating in the water settling amongst the sand giving it a golden shimmer from the sunshine. The locals call the flakes fool's gold because the pyrite washes from the mountain during rainy season and settles in the sand. Superficially the mineral looks like gold, and tourists sometimes think it's real. My mind flashed backed to the night of Kathy and Kadin's drowning and the painting of golden splendor I had been inspired to paint at the time of their death. The gold was a striking glitzy presence on this beach- and treasured on my painting.

I took time, walking the sandy beach alone, and ambled along the oceans lip silently praying. The water was chilly as it lapped and flowed over my feet. The sand glittered between my toes and outlined the footprints I left behind. Looking up at the Sierra Madrid Mountains, I saw heavenly haze formed atop them, which looked like the white murk mix also from my painting.

A tear ran down my cheek and mixed with the waves of the high tide. When the seawater retreated, my salty tear mixed together with the emerging emotional ocean forming and swelling inside me.

I sat back in a reclining chair soaking up the sun's warmth and experienced graphic flashbacks of my sister and nephew with new vivid visions of them in blissful peace with God. I went again to the water's rim and picked up a piece of driftwood. Kneeling in the sand I made my first mark to spell out ...K a t h y… K a d i n…

I dwelled and daydreamed on the indented sand words and I remembered watching Kathy carve the number "40" in the sand while I took her picture on our last trip. Eventually the letters I had dug into the sand began to wash away with the waves. How symbolic, watching their names melt into the sand, in time becoming indecipherable as the water washed their names from the earth. The ocean had ultimately laid claim to the golden sand.

Grief's sadness was mounting inside me...

I pulled a white lounge chair through the soft sand leaving a trail as I searched to shield myself from the hot sun. A tall, shady palm provided a respite as the emotions were coming over me now like the ocean waves, hard and fast. My throat was threatening to choke me. I felt intense gut-wrenching knots building, restricting needed air, if I didn't give in this time to releasing the pain of grief.

This was it.

I was going to lose it …and cry.

That or I was going to pass out from perhaps a heat stroke? No mistaking this alarming feeling. I was about to cry - hard, and I could do nothing to control or stop it. I felt a pervading heat travel over my chest, up my neck.

The culmination of all the memories, medications, moments of life with and without Kathy and Kadin were swelling inside. How I missed them both so much.

Every single day…

In a fixed gaze, I looked out at the crashing ocean and pulled down my dark-tinted sunglasses. The breaking surf hit the sandy shore as stored tears welled in my eyes, and burst.

Tears were now freely streaming beneath my sunspecs. It had taken me thousands of miles to an ocean paradise, to finally give in to genuine tears of mourning. I took in a several deep breaths and completely let all the air in my lungs out as if giving in to the biggest sigh ever.

Finally, I let go of the sadness… loss… grief.

It wasn't a long cry, but it was soul cleansing. I hoped the true tears of sorrow that I had denied myself to experience would begin a renaissance inside me once they were free. I was now unbound from the emotional pain that entrenched within me once I made the complete surrender to realize my loss. The stronghold of grief was broken.

I had an overwhelming sense that I could give myself permission to mentally move forward now. It was a relieving sensation. I was going to be OK. What a perfect place to be. I would not move on in my life as to forget them and what happened a year ago. I would let go and let God fill me on this beach, and He did.

For the past year, I had endured mental torture because I didn't want to feel. I didn't want to feel joy in my life, happiness, or pleasure. I welcomed self-inflicted misery. It had become so easy to accept and crave un-pleasantries. I was bearing heavy guilt for being alive. Yet, here, on this beach crying, I began to experience peace. Had I actually given in to grief? I knew I really had. The insanity of grieving the past year was melting away from my frozen heart, and it was OK.

I was melancholy to leave my tropical place of -resting in peace. One thing is for sure - memories and sad feelings find you wherever you go. There is no escaping. You can't hide from grief. Confront grief because dealing brings healing even if it takes time to find the strength to move on.

CHAPTER 21

Thawing

For what is it to die, but to stand in the sun and melt into the wind? -Khalil Gibran/Poet

Once my friend and I returned to the states from the grief retreat, I unexpectedly found myself much more emotionally composed. Despite my past misgivings about seeking professional help, I put faith and trust in another psychiatrist who was highly recommended by my counselor because he took sibling grief seriously. Even though I started to release my emotions on my grief getaway, I knew I needed continued support to move toward fully healing.

The new doctor listened and then prescribed different medications in combinations until the right formula was found that placed me chemically and emotionally in balance.

As part of my new balance, I gathered up most of the revered keepsakes of Kathy, Kadin, and my mom, that decorated my home everywhere and I created a sacred space for myself to spend time alone when I was downhearted.

I converted a walk-in closet to be my personal refuge. Now I had a treasured place to arrange piles of photos of my sister, Kadin, my mother, and grandparents so I could shuffle through them when I felt a little blue and wanted to reminisce.

For seating, I placed a black beanbag chair in my space. When I was in seventh grade, I was given a beanbag chair for Christmas. I always enjoyed reading, talking on the phone, and listening to my records with my jumbo-sized headphones while sitting comfortably in my cozy beanbag chair. Now 30 years later, I had been thoughtfully gifted another beanbag chair just perfect for my reflection spot.

My space is a place for keeping their memories close to me. I can sit and relax, pray, talk to them, and cry if I must. I admit, on some days I find it difficult to even open the door because the emotions are overwhelming. But I have the choice…to open the door and go in.

* * *

When, after some time, I started to fully accept their sudden deaths, I realized I never wished another family to needlessly suffer the heartbreak of losing loved ones from falling through thin ice and drowning. Every sequence of events from that evening they died plays out in my thoughts and sends my mind reeling.

When Kathy and I were younger, there was a pond across the field from our house we would ice skate on. We didn't know any danger existed.

What if the boys **had** learned about the danger of ice and drowning? Would they all be alive?

Ice safety information geared to educate kids about ice and drowning was absent in our community and barely found on the Internet with much searching effort. All children needed an easy way to comprehend lifesaving information on the web, but it was aimed for adults. The education needed to be more than just telling kids "Don't go on the ice." Something more needed to be done.

My cousin and her daughter felt called to action and had the initial idea of raising ice awareness. A small group of relatives and friends came together because it would take my family and friends' combined efforts to launch such an undertaking. We formed a not-for-profit corporation called Project Skipper®.

Developing an ice safety program for kids would involve fundraising, visibility in the community, and telling the story of three lives lost. I knew that I wouldn't be emotionally ready to be overly active at the start because I was just coming to grips with my deep loss. "Maybe this project, by helping kids learn the danger, is what I need to move my grief further along?" I contemplated. I decided to give the enormous effort a try, not really sure if I was ready for the emotional commitment of educating kids on ice and drowning.

Talking with school groups, troops of boy and girl scouts, and raising awareness at health and safety fairs with our ice education booths has brought me peace of mind. When I talk with kids and they raise their hands that they have heard of Project Skipper and ice dangers I know our educational efforts are making an impact.

CHAPTER 22

A love that never dies

There is sacredness in tears. They are not the mark of weakness, but of power. They speak more eloquently than ten thousand tongues. They are messengers of overwhelming grief ...and unspeakable love.

Washington Irvin ~ Author

Fresh grass clippings clung to my leather sandals. I toted flowery arrangements and foliage, Styrofoam, and some thin wire in my trash bag as I unhurriedly sidestepped the gravestones. The breeze was calm, and I noticed on the tall pole the American flag was gesturing as if it were waving "good day," stirred by the gentle wind, pleased to see me visit once again.

As I meandered along, I felt the sun's rays warm my face. I remembered a time not so long ago where I chose to have my skin remain pale, peaked, pasty and avoided being out in the sun, avoided the light. Avoided the comfort the light could bring. Gods light.

The black marble stone shimmered as the sun's rays peered brightly through the clouds overhead. I continued looking down at the memorial, still amazed every time I read their names, KATHY ANN BAXMEYER nee KOHLER, KADIN JOHN BAXMEYER that they both are departed.

It is real.

Set in stone.

I gave a protracted sigh, and started a one-sided conversation while I tidied up the gravesite. I kicked the freshly mowed grass from around the stone's base, and clanked the hanging wind chimes, re-arranged a horseshoe, a small angel statue, and a butterfly garden ornament, giving them a fresher prominence. The sun-faded artificial flowers in the pair of twin marble vases were interchanged with new colorful flowers, complete with wired ribbons and bows. "Sis, hope you like these white and red roses," and "Kadin, here are some plastic green Army men," I remarked, as I placed some of the men in formation on the headstone's edge.

Down the row of stones to the right of their resting place is a plot not yet in use. Grass and dots of yellow dandelions cover the spot. Someday, I will be resting next to Kathy and Kadin for the unused plot … is mine.

I lingered as my mind reviewed how painfully intense and unsettling to my soul losing both Kathy and Kadin so suddenly was for me. The feelings of hopeless depression, being alone, fear of the future were so severe I needed professional counseling and medication to bring about a more positive outlook on life. I first viewed myself as weak for needing therapy. What I have come to appreciate is that grief can make you feel many feelings or not feel at all. I'm definitely not the same person I was before their deaths, but I'm stronger. Overcome the despair by seeking out those who can make you stronger.

Reaching peace within eventually became my desire, but I couldn't imagine ever fully attaining that goal. The inner peace I longed desperately for came because of a renewed, reawakened faith and ultimate surrender, allowing others, including my Christian counselor, to come into my life and walk with me on my streets of sorrow. I had to grieve their loss but also grieve the unfulfilled dreams and future without them.

Do not side step grief. I tried to put off grieving in the short term. Unfortunately, by not honestly dealing with my painful loss, I found that grief grew and shadowed me wherever I went. Reflecting over the past years, I now understand just how much worry I caused those who loved me most. I have regrets for that. I needed to allow them to be a part of my grief process, but instead I pushed them away. Certainly, there was fluctuating sadness, but I needed to be willing to accept comfort from those around me.

Return to church. Although it took me some time to start attending church services again, I appreciate now how God uses others to help me heal even when I feel alone as a sibling griever. Find and get into a support group.

As I walked along the rows, I knew there would always be emotional prompts I couldn't escape. Events such as birthdays, holidays, or other special shared days would bring me both glad and sad memories. Memories come when and where I may least expect it, but I do expect it.

Still in profound thought, I replaced the worn flowers from my grandmother and grandfather's headstones and worked my way to my mother's place of rest.

Dealing with my tragic sibling loss and loss of my nephew made me incredibly withdrawn and miserable. I had lost irreplaceable and important family who were so incredibly dear to me. The possibility of an outflow of untimely, unexpected tears where I wasn't anticipating a crying session has made me thankful I had a full tissue box handy! I'd cry copiously on some days when I was alone, and remarkably find pleasure and laughter on others. I felt those mixed-up emotions, but to regain a balance, I needed to allow myself to experience joy and gladness, along with the sadness.

With a full trash bag of faded flowers, I headed for my car. Passing other graves, I noticed many monuments without flowers and wondered if anyone ever stopped there…

Everyone grieves in different fashions. This has been my case. With my grief avoidance I wanted to keep them alive and holding onto the pain became a connection to them. Now, I hold the perfect beautiful memories close in my heart and mind, not the ugly pain.

Grief is really hard work!

I chose to remain frozen from my intense grief because the thawing, I thought, would be unbearable. Staying frozen with my feelings, not venting, gave me needed control. I thought it was easier denying my deep hurt, pretending to be fine, than embracing the pain and learning, growing from it.

Release your hurt.

Plan that grief vacation. Find a sacred space, like I did, to recognize your sadness and acknowledge your loss - your void.

Melting the grief I held onto has been a slow process and has changed over time. I have to reestablish my place in this world. Take the time you need to grieve, the time you need to thaw.

Grief shouldn't have any rules…any timetable.

My complicated loss will take me a lifetime to come to terms with- but I'm working on recognizing my healing needs. I do expect emotional meltdowns, but life is becoming clearer. I am more at peace as I am being restored.

How I miss my relatives- my Mom, Kathy, and Kadin, every single day. But for certain I know: Happy memories and the true love for them I hold close remains, even though they are gone. The memories of family, my sister and Kadin are…mine, and are some of the most precious and wonderful to me.

When I reached my car I turned back again facing all my family monuments and gave a small wave goodbye putting them to rest. I had my moment of peace and stood motionless with a watery tear forming in the corner of my eye.

Appendix : Ice Education

Project Skipper ® is a not-for-profit corporation that promotes ice safety education and raises awareness of the dangers of ice-covered bodies of water and drowning, and teaches simplified self-rescue techniques. The project's main message stresses to children to **never go out on ice** at all, instead, go to a supervised ice rink.

But, if something unanticipated happens and a child finds themselves falling through ice and into water, there are simple steps that the child can take to help save themselves from drowning. The education program's foundation is adapted from frozen water skills taught to Navy seals, and other found information on cold water survival techniques aimed for adults from a leading Canadian professor. We teach a kid-friendly version, which can be easily remember. Kids really need the ice education

Skipper is the mascot, a little boy. The letters S.K.P.R. are an abbreviation for the safety steps to follow once you fall through the ice into the water. We teach the kids that the "**S**" stands for, staying calm and not panicking. During an educational class, kids put their hands in a large bucket of ice cubes and water. They typically shout out, "It's so cold."

Yes, the icy water is very cold, but we teach them that staying calm can help them think and save themselves from going beneath the water and drowning.

The **"K"** is for kicking the legs and feet. Once the child enters the water after falling through the ice, kicking will keep the body parallel to the ice opening. This kicking like a swimmer puts the body in a better position to prop and pull onto the ice edge and out of the water.

The "**P**" stands for pulling up and out onto the solid ice. Pulling while kicking will help to propel your body out of the water. Keep kicking and pulling, kicking and pulling while propping elbows onto the ice edge. After you exit the water do not stand up! You may just fall right back into danger again.

Finally, the "**R**" is for rolling away from the danger. Lie down on the ice after pulling out of the water and roll with arms tucked into your side to distribute your weight more evenly. Roll all the way to the safety of the shore. Then stand up and go for help and tell someone you fell into cold water.

During the programs I have been blessed to give, I have heard several responses from the kids that they "know about a mom and two little boys who drowned."

My heart always skips several beats.

I may never know if the steps have saved a life, but talking with parents and kids to raise awareness has been personally worthwhile, yet remains "heart" challenging. It will always anguish me to recognize how vital our now learned ice safety information could have been as a lifesaver for the two boys and my sister if it had been developed sooner. Then maybe the boys could have been introduced early in school to stay off ice through our lesson plans. This project is a work in progress and has been a healing pathway for me and for my family. My sister was so brave to enter the water in a heroic effort, but what if she had known more about ice safety?

Kids are naturally drawn to frozen water, and they might not just stay off the ice when their guardians tell them to do so. My daughter authored a children's book on ice safety and I illustrated it for her. *See Ice, Think Twice A Story about Ice Safety,* is a kid- friendly book aimed at young learners. Perhaps, a child might read the book and start a conversation with their parents. The educational book is dedicated to Kathy and Kadin's memory and is available on Amazon.com.

About the Author

Karen Kohler Kaiser is an adult sibling survivor of sudden grief who resides in Illinois. Her past published works include feature articles and a monthly column in a dental trade magazine spanning a decade. She currently practices dental hygiene and continues to paint. To see her creative works or contact Karen visit www. karenkohlerkaiser com

About the Cover

Artist: Karen Kohler Kaiser
Original Painting -Mixed Media Acrylics
Title- ***At the Time of Death***

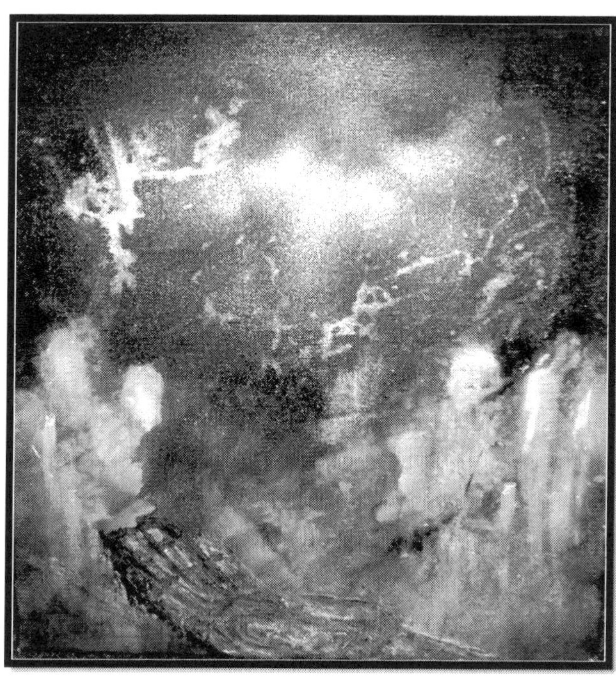

"Every artist dips his brush in his soul, and paints his nature into his pictures."

Henry Ward Beecher

This book was written by this author to the best of her knowledge regarding truthful events reflecting on her own death and grief circumstances. The author has no background in grief counseling. She does have personal experiences. This book is not intended as a substitute for professional counseling therapy but rather to allow the readers to experience a grief process about the sudden deaths of loved ones. Any information provided for ice safety is intended to educate and is to be used at the discretion of the reader.

Made in the USA
Lexington, KY
25 October 2014